# Hearts Afire

Books by Vance Havner

# Hearts Afire

by

## VANCE HAVNER

## FLEMING H. REVELL COMPANY

### WESTWOOD, N. J.

#### LOS ANGELES   LONDON   GLASGOW

WESTWOOD, N. J.—316 THIRD AVENUE
LOS ANGELES 41—2173 COLORADO BOULEVARD
LONDON E. C., 4—29 LUDGATE HILL
GLASGOW C. 2—229 BOTHWELL STREET

# Contents

# Foreword

These messages have been given all over the land and some have appeared in various Christian publications. They endeavor to strike the same note the writer has tried to sound through the years, and it is hoped that at no point will the trumpet give an uncertain sound, for it is high time that every soldier of Christ prepare himself for the battle.

It is an age of itching ears. What we need is burning hearts. We need a heart-warming!

*Greensboro, N. C.*                                    *V. H.*

# 1

# Hearts Afire

*But his word was in mine heart as a burning fire shut up in my bones, and I was weary with forbearing and I could not stay.*

JEREMIAH 20:9.

*Did not our heart burn within us while he talked with us by the way and while he opened to us the scriptures?*

LUKE 24:32.

THOSE OF US WHO ARE TEMPTED TO GET UNDER THE juniper because of the condition of the church might do well to ponder the spiritual state of England two hundred years ago. It was a dark hour. As someone has put it, "The Puritans had been buried and the Methodists were not yet born." In one section only one Bible could be found and that was used to prop up a flower-pot. It was publicly advertised in front of drinking places that one could get drunk for one penny and dead drunk for two. France had gone into infidelity and England would have followed had not a young preacher on May 24, 1738, attended a meeting on Aldersgate Street and felt his own heart strangely warmed.

The course of a nation was changed because one preacher had a heart-warming. John Wesley did more

to make England over than all the experts and re-
formers. This old world is in a sad way now, and lately
it has almost been wrecked by hotheads. The only
hope, as in Wesley's day, is a spiritual revival, and that
calls, not for hot heads, of which we have a plenty even
in the church, but for hot hearts.

You recognize the texts. In the first, Jeremiah is
ready to quit preaching. He is like that preacher who
wanted to resign but who was impressed within that
what he needed was not to resign but to have his commission re-signed. He tried to quit but couldn't. He
developed a bone-fire. Here was a prophet with a holy
fever, a preacher running a spiritual temperature, a
man of God with a burning heart.

The other text brings us to the Emmaus disciples
after those exciting crucifixion days in Jerusalem.
They were trudging along a country road, half-believ-
ing, half-doubting, suffering a let-down both in body
and spirit, when the Lord caught up with them. They
were right in their facts: "This is the third day." But
they were wrong in their conclusions, for, since it was
the third day, they should have been expecting to see
the risen Christ around any bend of the road. They
were right in their chronology and in their theology,
but they had no doxology. And even when the Lord
did appear, their eyes were holden, He was a veiled
Christ. But when He expounded the Scriptures they
developed a holy heartburn, which led to an experience that stirred their hearts and turned them into
radiant witnesses.

Their plight before their hearts were warmed is
typical of thousands of orthodox Christians today. At
the bottom of all our troubles lies unreality in our

Christian experience. We are walking with a veiled Christ. We need a holy heartburn.

A. J. Gordon once classified some obstreperous church members as "figureheads, soreheads and deadheads." He might have added "hotheads," of which there is always an abundance. But a man may have a hot head and a cold heart. Christmas Evans, just out of a theological controversy, was convicted of a cold heart as he rode along through the mountains one Saturday afternoon, traveling on horseback to preach next day. Great preacher that he was, he needed a heart-warming and got it after hours in prayer.

Alexander Whyte was wont to watch the radiant throngs that emerged from Mr. Moody's great meetings in those Pentecostal days during the mission to the British Isles. Their hearts had been warmed by the ministry of the Spirit. Mr. Moody went to Scotland some years after the Disruption and found the churches cold and divided. But he did not go to Scotland as an expert; he went as an evangelist, exulting in the grace of God. A witness said, "It seemed as though someone had set to music a tune that had been haunting thousands of ears." He warmed their hearts.

One thinks of the professor who wrote a very learned book on love. The only defect was, the professor had never been in love. When he took the manuscript to a typist to have it prepared for the publisher, the typist turned out to be a very lovely lady, and when their eyes met something happened to the professor that was not in the book. He was happier in five minutes with love in his heart than he had been in thirty years with love in his head.

Something like that needs to happen to a lot of fundamentalists. Some of our churches are frozen together when they should be melted together. We have plenty of orthodoxy, plenty of teaching, plenty of activity; there is an abundance of good things, and in the midst of it all we are like a cat drowning in cream. There is plenty of discussion of revivals, causes of revival, hindrances to revival, ways and means of revival: the only thing lacking is revival. We agree that it is the work of the Spirit, but here again we spend our time arguing over the expressions and missing the experience. Baptism, filling, enduement, victorious life, perfect love, full surrender—we are like a crowd of beggars discussing the merits of different kinds of pocketbooks and all of them "broke"!

We are afraid of extremism, until we are guilty of the worst extremism of all, the extremism of impotence. Some of us are so afraid that we shall "get out on a limb" that we never get up the tree! Whatever you choose to call it, we need a heart-warming, a heavenly bone-fire, a holy heartburn. Our heads and hands have outrun our hearts. We have forgotten that the way forward is not head first but heart first. We have been wagging our heads and working our hands instead of warming our hearts.

To be "fervent in spirit" is to be "boiling in spirit," and to boil we must be near the Fire. How shall we obtain the burning heart? Jeremiah said it was God's Word that did it and it was Jesus expounding the Scriptures that did it and it was while listening to Luther's exposition of Romans that Wesley's heart was warmed. There is, indeed, the strange fire that Nadab and Abihu offered instead of supernatural fire from above. There is the false fire of Isaiah 50:11: "Behold, all ye that kindle a fire, that compass yourselves about with sparks: walk in the light of your fire, and in the sparks that ye have kindled. This shall ye have of mine hand, ye shall lie down in sorrow." There is the Divine Fire which is the gift of God, and this fire Paul urged Timothy to stir up within him. Every Christian has the Holy Spirit, but the fire often dies down, and he must needs wait on God through the Word and prayer and rekindle the flame until the love of God is shed afresh in his heart, for, like Ephesus of old, we leave our first love, and because iniquity abounds our love grows cold. It takes time to do that, not because God is reluctant but because we are rebellious. It takes effort, for we must apply the means of grace. But if instead of trying to work up carnal enthusiasm and whip up our poor jaded nerves with religious excitement, we took time out to really get ourselves a burning heart we would accomplish more in a day than we get done in a year without it.

Much of our Christianity today is like the feast at Cana when it ran out of wine. We have a feast of good things: there is plenty of teaching and preaching; churches and conferences spread tables loaded with superabundance. But we have no wine. The exhilaration of the Spirit is lacking. The spiritual wine that makes glad the heart of man is gone. We need a heart-warming!

John the Baptist was not to drink wine, but he was to be filled with the Spirit. On the day of Pentecost the church was accused of being drunk on new wine, when it was really Spirit-filled. We are not to be drunk with wine but filled with the Spirit. There is a parallel between the two. Campbell Morgan asks: "Has anyone ever charged you with being drunk with your Christianity? O God, how seldom men have thought us drunk!"

Art, literature, statesmanship, scientific discoveries are the work of drunk men. We see the principle perverted in the drunkard and the dope fiend or in a Hitler. We see the constructive side in a Beethoven, an Edison, a Lincoln. Even as children we are "drunk on the wine of youth." A little later we get drunk on love. What man does not remember some summer night when he was so in love that he loved the moon and stars and everybody except that rival who was running him a close race for the heart of his beloved? Why do we Christians not so love Jesus until we love everybody except the arch enemy of our souls?

Now, just as the natural man has his stimulants, good and bad, so has the Christian. We have meat to eat and also wine to drink that the world knows not of. Our wine is the Spirit, and yet most of us are not drunk Christians. We need our hearts warmed. When George Fox was going through his spiritual crisis, he was advised to drink beer. His advisers sensed a need but could not supply the remedy. Later he got drunk on the wine of heaven and warmed up many another soul thereafter.

Our world is drunk. Some Christians are drunk on false wine, having fired themselves with the energy of the flesh. It will take the true wine of the Spirit to move this world. God has provided a heart-warmer for His people: "Be not drunk with wine, wherein is excess; *but be filled with the Spirit.*" And, unlike the wines of earth, there is no hangover: "The blessing of the Lord it maketh rich and he addeth no sorrow with it." There is no dark-brown, morning-after taste to the joy of the Lord!

We have run out of wine. But there was one at Cana who could meet the emergency. "Whatsoever he saith unto you, do it." He can meet our need. If we take Him at His word and fill the waterpots with water, He will work His miracle, and those to whom we minister will say that the last wine is better than the first!

We shall never warm our hearts until we gather around the Lord. Only a Person, Christ Himself, unites us. There are conservative Christians who wouldn't be caught on the same platform. All our plans for getting them together move so slowly because they won't jell! The only place where we can get together is where we are already together, in Him.

We need a holy heartburn. Our eyes are holden. We need a fresh experience of the reality of Jesus Christ.

> Lord Jesus, make Thyself to me
> A living, bright Reality;
> More pleasant to faith's vision keen
> Than any outward object seen,
> More dear, more intimately nigh,
> Than e'en the sweetest earthly tie.

We need to forget which group we belong to, which movement we are sponsoring, which button we are wearing, which Paul or Apollos or Cephas we are lined up with, long enough to ask, "Is Jesus real to me?" Is He real to you? Is your heart warm? He told us the secret: "He that hath my commandments, and keepeth them, he it is that loveth me: and he that loveth me shall be loved of my Father, and I will love

him, *and will manifest myself to him*" (John 14:21).
How was He made real to these Emmaus disciples?
When He overtook them, they had burdened hearts;
then they had burning hearts, and when they recognized Him they had believing hearts. Well, they invited Him in as their guest, and He became their host.
He was always doing that. At Cana He was first the
guest, and, when the wine gave out, He became the
host. Again He says, "Behold, I stand at the door and
knock; if any man hear my voice, and open the door, I
will come in to him, and will sup with him"—"I'll be
his guest—and he with me—He'll be my guest." The
Emmaus disciples took Him in and then the guest became host and made Himself known and sent them out
to witness to others.

Has He taken over in your heart? Perhaps He resides
there, but does He preside? Or maybe you have never
opened the door. Prebendary Webb-Peploe used to say,
"Sometimes I buy a present for my wife. I am afraid
that my selections are often very poor, but she always
accepts them graciously, because she knows that before
I ever gave her these presents I gave her my heart."
Now, all the roses and jewels there are can never make
a wife happy if she knows her husband has not first
given her his heart. Nor can all our gifts and religious
observances please our Lord until first we give Him
ourselves.

Let Him take over, and He will give you a heavenly
bone-fire and holy heartburn, and will rekindle your
heart with fire from above.

> May Thy rich grace impart
> Strength to my fainting heart,
> My zeal inspire;

As Thou hast died for me,
O may my love to Thee
Pure, warm and changeless be,
A living fire!

From "My Faith Looks Up
To Thee," by Ray Palmer.

# 2

# On Being Faithful

*Let a man so account of us, as of the ministers of Christ, and stewards of the mysteries of God. Moreover it is required in stewards, that a man be found faithful. But with me it is a very small thing that I should be judged of you, or of man's judgment: yea, I judge not mine own self. For I know nothing by myself; yet am I not hereby justified: but he that judgeth me is the Lord. Therefore judge nothing before the time, until the Lord come, who both will bring to light the hidden things of darkness, and will make manifest counsels of the hearts: and then shall every man have praise of God.*

I CORINTHIANS 4:1–5.

ONE MIGHT CALL THESE VERSES A PREACHER'S DECLARA-tion of Independence. Paul speaks of three bars before which a minister's work appears: private judgment, public opinion, and Divine justice. A preacher judges himself, he is judged of others, he will finally be judged of God. What matters most is that final judgment, for "to his own master he standeth or falleth." Paul did not worry about what people thought of his ministry. He realized that he was not capable of measuring it properly himself. When our Lord sent His disciples out to preach, they returned and reported to Christ, not to a committee. So we are to report one day to the

Judge Himself, and He will appraise our work and that day shall declare it.

The text is verse two: "Moreover it is required in stewards that a man be found faithful." Two words stand out, "steward," and "faithful." Verse 1 says that we are stewards of the mysteries of God. A mystery in the New Testament is not a glorified puzzle but rather something which we never would have known had not the Holy Spirit revealed it. "And without controversy great is the mystery of godliness: God was manifest in the flesh, justified in the Spirit, seen of angels, preached unto the Gentiles, believed on in the world, received up into glory" (I Tim. 3:16). We are stewards of that glorious mystery, "stewards of the manifold grace of God," as Peter puts it. The word "steward" means a householder; it reminds us of our Saviour's word: "Every scribe instructed unto the kingdom of heaven is like unto a man that is an householder, which bringeth forth out of his treasure things new and old" (Mt. 13:52).

One may think of a minister as a householder standing before the people with all the treasure of God behind him, giving out of that wealth with never a fear of a Mother Hubbard experience, for that cupboard will never be bare! He is not a depository but a dispenser. And we are all stewards, not of our money alone, as so many understand stewardship, but of time and talents, all we are and all we have.

It is required in such stewards that they be found faithful, trustworthy. The Word of God puts high value on old-fashioned faithfulness. Certainly "God is faithful" (I Cor. 1:9; 10:13); "Faithful is he that calleth you" (I Thess. 5:24); "The Lord is faithful"

(II Thess. 3:3); "He is faithful that promised" (Heb. 10:23).

God is faithful, and He expects His people to be faithful. God's faithfulness does not excuse us from our obligation, for "it is required" of us that we be faithful. God's Word speaks of faithful servants, faithful in a few things, faithful in the least, faithful in the Lord, faithful ministers. And all points up that day when He will say, "Well done, thou good and faithful servant."

In John we read that many believed on Jesus when they saw His miracles but that He did not believe in them. We have a song, "Can the Lord Depend on You?" It ought to be sung more often. John wrote to Gaius, "Thou doest *faithfully* whatsoever thou doest. . . ." Gaius was not fitful or flashy, he was faithful. It has been said that the greatest ability is dependability. There is not much preaching on old-fashioned faithfulness. Perhaps one reason is that faithfulness is not very glamorous. If a wife murders her husband, that gets into all the papers. But there are thousands of faithful wives and mother who never get the spotlight, who grace their homes with loving service, whose husbands and children rise up to call them blessed.

What a terrible time we have in our churches trying to keep people faithful in attendance and loyalty! How we reward and picnic and coax and tantalize church members into doing things they don't want to do but which they would do if they loved God! The only service that counts is faithful service that issues from love of Christ. The choir singer who does not sing from the heart should get right or get out. True faith shows up in faithfulness.

The work of the pastor is frowned upon in many quarters because it calls for faithfulness in a daily grind of unromantic, colorless duties, and some try to sidestep that by moving into more exciting activities.

Christian living calls for faithfulness. Not every one can sing or preach, but all can be faithful. Maybe that is what takes the glamour out of it—anybody can do it! Anyway, there isn't much of it. Too many saints go up like rockets and come down like rocks. They prefer to be flashy comets instead of faithful stars. But God prefers those who faithfully let their light shine to those who fitfully show it. It is better not to shine so dazzlingly at one time but rather to shine daily, all the time.

This is the Age of Goofus, of trickery, hocus-pocus, freaks, sleight-of-hand, "now-you-see-it-and-now-you-don't." Everything is done with mirrors. Everything is measured by "How big?" and "How loud?" Everything must be huge, gigantic, colossal, super-duper. Even the new drugs are "wonder drugs"—you take them and wonder what will happen next. In such a time it is hard to interest people in plain old obedience and faithfulness. Even Christians must be entertained at church. The Light of Truth is looked at but not walked in, and, being hearers but nor doers, men are blinded by excess of light. Too much light will blind as surely as not enough light.

God's Word has much to say about being steadfast, grounded, settled, built on a rock, not carried about with every wind of doctrine. We are not to be weary in well-doing. We ought to be able to say, "My heart is fixed." Of course, some saints are permanent fixtures, but our permanence should be the living permanence

of a tree, not the dead stability of a tombstone. Too
many restless Christians today move from church to
church, preacher to preacher, always getting right and
never getting right, ever learning but never able to
come to a knowledge of the truth. Some are always lay-
ing foundations but never building thereon. Others
are "hypodermic saints," living on shots of religious
excitement instead of growing normally by food, rest,
and exercise. Unless some stabilization is mixed with
our salvation, we are going to have a generation of pop-
corn Christians, popping all over the place.

It is required of stewards that they be found faithful,
not fitful. And we are to be faithful over a few things.
The preacher who will not preach his heart out before
a few people would be no good before a multitude.
There are too many eagles on hummingbird nests, too
big for their present location and seeking great things
for themselves, as did Baruch of old.

This unfaithfulness shows up at church. Too many
saints have no local loyalty. They will support a radio
preacher at a distance, which is well enough in its
place, but will not help a man of God in their own
community. He may not be brilliant or well-known,
but God did not call him to be that; God called him to
be faithful, and if he is faithful we ought to be faithful to him. Away with that view of the invisible church
that makes a man invisible at church on Sunday!

Such unfaithfulness shows up at home. It is force-
fully enjoined upon bishops and deacons that they be
faithful at home; and it is expected of the rest of us.
It avails nothing to look pious at the Lord's table on
Sunday if we show no grace at the breakfast table
through the week. It is not well in many Christian

homes today with husband, wife or child. There needs to be fresh affirmation of Joshua's resolve: "As for me and my house, we will serve the Lord."

Back of unfaithfulness to church and home lies heart unfaithfulness to Christ. Our God is a jealous God, and when His people were untrue He called it adultery. We Christians are married to Christ (Rom. 7:4), we bear His name. Paul was jealous over his flock with a godly jealousy, for he had espoused them to one husband as a chaste virgin to Christ. James writes to believers: "Ye adulterers and adulteresses, know ye not that the friendship of the world is enmity with God? Whosoever therefore will be a friend of the world is the enemy of God." When we are untrue to Christ we bring reproach on that holy Name by which we are called. If we are in love with Christ, we will be true all down the line, to ourselves, to the home, to church; with our time, talents, money. Jesus did not ask Peter, "Lovest thou feeding sheep?" or "Lovest thou sheep?" but "Lovest thou me?"

Are you a faithful steward? The Judge is coming, and he will reward every man according to his work. Are you ready to give account of your stewardship? Two little girls in school were excited about the forthcoming visit of the school board. "You'd better clean up your desk, for they might come any time," suggested one.

"I'll clean it up tomorrow."
"But they might come today."
"I'll clean it up this afternoon."
"But they might come this morning."
"I guess I'll keep it clean all the time!"

What does your desk look like? Is there a lot of un-
finished business on it? Are you up to date with your
Bible and prayer? Are there some things between you
and others that ought to be straightened out?

The Judge may come at any time to check with His
stewards. And it is required of stewards that they be
found faithful.

# 3

# A Good Word for "The Good Old Days"

THESE LATTER YEARS HAVE WITNESSED A RASH OF BOOKS depicting the old parlor-lamp and family-album days of a generation now gone. These writers have not dealt kindly with the faith of their fathers. Human frailty in pulpit and pew has been exploited, and, in an effort to produce racy reading, liberties have been taken with the holiest matters. It is to be feared that fools have rushed in where angels fear to tread.

It is very fashionable nowadays for this age to give vent to long-suppressed resentment and rebellion by ridiculing the religious life of its elders. One would think, to read some of this muckraking, that all deacons and preachers were Pharisees. It would seem that any generation that has made as big a mess of things as has this one would be too red in the face to sling mud at its forebears. Back of some of it there may be a nostalgia and a suspicion that perhaps our elders really had something which our pride will not let us stoop to find. Then, of course, we have heard everything, read everything, experienced everything—except those secrets which are hidden from the wise and prudent and revealed unto babes. Even a knowledge of the good may keep us from knowing the best. Knowing too much, we do not know enough.

This writer can hold his own with any of the scribblers so far as a countrified background is concerned. I did not grow up in a parsonage, but my father's house almost amounted to one. He was called to preach, but he didn't, and for the rest of his life he felt that he had missed his calling. He worked doubly hard trying to make up for some of it on second bests. For one thing, his home was open to preachers, and they seemed to gravitate to our "prophet's chamber." We had a blessing at every meal, family prayers at night. Father was a strict disciplinarian. His thumbs were down on movies, cards, dancing. Although he lived on a farm he looked more like a preacher, wore a white collar and derby hat. His garb seemed to suggest the minister he should have been. His church work at old Corinth came first. Bee-keeping was his hobby. I was his greatest human interest. He lived over in me, and when I asked to be licensed to preach he was in seventh heaven.

If I were following the popular pattern I would digress at this point and begin poking fun at the narrow Puritanism of those days in contrast with this modern paradise of sweetness and light. I see no reason why I should do so. If I were going to have some fun, it would be at the expense of this present race of aspirin eaters hunting as feverishly as their stomach ulcers will allow for a hole in the ground where they can hide from their own inventions. At least, we could live on top of the ground in the old days. If Father thought the world was growing worse—and he did— he was a pretty good prophet. For further information, read any newspaper and listen to the radio—if you can.

I recall the revival meetings at old Corinth Church at "laying-by time," when the farmers had a little leisure. The church yard was filled with horses, mules, buggies, wagons. Once in a while some of the elite came in surreys. Hound dogs roamed here and there. Inside the church we hung kerosene lamps on the walls. There was the wheezy organ and singing from shaped-note books. Preaching was long and loud, with a call for mourners.

I do not defend all that happened. Sometimes much was made of the emotional appeal—meeting our loved ones in heaven, for instance. We sang songs with separate verses about father, mother, sister, brother, husband, wife, children. The pressure was pretty heavy. Some of the more stubborn held out, but you had to be pretty stubborn. At the mourners' bench instruction was not always clear. The penitent might be kneeling between two of the brethren, one exhorting him to "hold on" while the other urged him to "turn loose." Usually there was a crisis, when the seeker came through shouting, and sometimes walked all over the church shaking hands with everybody. We had some dear souls who always went into a shout when the spiritual temperature reached a certain point. My grandmother shouted through the Baptist revival one week and the Methodist revival next week, year after year, and the denomination didn't matter when she really "got happy." One sister used to go up and down the aisles shouting with her eyes shut, and never did hit a bench. I don't know how she did it.

Yes, I know that some of the converts didn't "stick," but most of them did. Those who did stick are grandparents now, and grace has brought them across many

a rough mile since. I do know that after a rousing
morning service when people were converted, we went
home that day feeling fresh and clean inside. "Heaven
above was softer blue, earth around was sweeter
green," and our humdrum lives had been touched with
the light of a better world. And when we came back
at "early candle-light" for night "preachin'" those
plain old faces had something written on them that I
don't read on the countenances I scan in hotel lobbies
and Pullman lounge cars these days.

There came a time when I returned to old Corinth
and smiled condescendingly at the mourners and
shouters, who were becoming fewer by then. I thought
I had advanced into intellectual realms beyond such
primitive ways. I can understand some of the stuff I
read now that laughs at hill-billy religion. It reminds
me of when I was reading Elbert Hubbard, trying to
wear a flowing tie and be a free-lance writer. It took
me a long time to learn that the Bible means what it
says when it declares that we must become fools to be
wise. We either become fools God's way or stay fools
our way.

I wasted several years dabbling in more liberal views.
The worst of that is, it does not satisfy, and yet ninety-
nine out of a hundred are not willing to admit they are
wrong and go back to the old paths. I have found
nothing that works except the simple faith in Jesus
Christ that obeys Him in loving service. I am no ad-
vocate of the orgies now abounding in some store-front
churches and among religion's lunatic fringe. But the
big church folk lost something when they let the little
churches across the railroad tracks produce all the hal-

lelujahs and amens. I have never shouted in public, but I see no reason why all the exuberance should be found at political rallies and ball games.

And what was wrong with the old method of scaring the ungodly with a sermon on hell? My father was jolted loose from his lethargy by a hair-raising, blood-curdling treatment of the text, "He that being often reproved hardeneth his neck shall suddenly be destroyed and that without remedy." Such a sermon would horrify the delicate sensibilities of a modern "refined" audience that can enjoy the filth of a theater or wade through the corruption of some best-sellers but cannot endure sound doctrine from the pulpit. But that discourse landed my father in the Kingdom of God and made him a moral and spiritual force in his community for the rest of his days. I am thankful that a preacher scared him into heaven instead of lulling him into hell.

As I have indicated, sometimes the very opposite of this method was employed, and sinners were urged to be converted that they might some day join their loved ones in heaven. Of course, there was a terrific pull in that appeal. We have gone the other way now, and sermons on heaven are as scarce as the proverbial hen's teeth. Some have long since ceased talking about the "land that is fairer than day" for fear of being called "celestial excursionists" living for "pie in the sky." I hear "survival of personality" but not heaven. Well, after the years have taken their toll and so many we loved dearly are congregated on the other side, the new skepticism affords us cold comfort. Those we have loved long since and lost awhile are somewhere, and folks who talk so much of the historic Jesus should remember that it was He who spoke most clearly on both hell and heaven.

Maybe one reason why some no longer sing, "There's A Land That Is Fairer Than Day" is because the next line says "And By Faith I Can See It Afar." You have to have faith to see it, and there isn't much of that nowadays. In fact, our Saviour left no doubt that He didn't expect to find much of it when He comes again.

If I were still among the unconverted, it would be smart, according to present standards, to blame my plight on the way I was brought up. More infidels than Bob Ingersoll have made much of a stern religious childhood. I passed through a period of reaction myself, but today I am preaching substantially the same doctrine my father believed and stood for, and I think he would say "amen" through any of my sermons. If I departed from it awhile, I returned to abide forever. I do not now think his standards were too high. From all I can see and hear of the life I miss by being a Christian I realize more and more that I haven't missed much.

I was not convinced of these spiritual realities at the end of an argument. Very few people are—on any subject. A lot of people simply don't want to be convinced because they don't want to give up their evil ways. No use arguing, something must happen on the inside.

That is the cure for all the cynicism that slurs the "good old days." I am not blind to the evils of those times and am painting no haloes for the old-timers. But what some of their critics need is just to be converted.

I would not waste time, breath or ink trying to out-argue them. There is a world that the humblest soul may know, while kings may never find it. No college degree will furnish the password nor can wealth buy us entrance. We get in by being born again, and that means a miracle and all that is foolishness to this age. Wherever there is one who will humble himself to prove it, it works just as it always works. But stiff necks and hard hearts find it too difficult to buck the horse-laugh of the cynics and be God's fools. It was difficult for a learned doctor to take it in when Jesus was on earth, but still the accents ring across the years from a still night long ago,

*Ye must be born again!*

# 4

# The Lift That Lasts

PETER AND JOHN WERE ON THEIR WAY TO THE TEMPLE, not to sacrifice, but to pray. I am not surprised that a wonderful thing happened that day. You are always on the highroad to a blessing when you are on your way to the house of God.

At the Beautiful Gate lay a man lame from his birth. Therefore, first of all in this story, we have a *lameness*. This man symbolizes a crippled world at the door of the church. Were there ever more cripples than now—crippled bodies, crippled minds, crippled lives, crippled homes? Two world wars have filled the earth with a crop of them. They fill our hospitals. They walk our streets. You do not always see the limp, for it may be a lameness of mind or heart. We live in a crippled world, groaning and travailing in pain. We are all cripples. Sorrow has done it. Sickness has done it. Sin has done it. Satan has done it.

This generation of lame men lies at the door of the church. Not that they go to church, for they don't, but they are our responsibility and their need is our challenge. Remember the father who brought his demonized boy to the disciples that they might cast out the demon, *and they could not*. But Jesus said, "Bring him to me." The disciples may fail, churches may fail,

32

but He does not fail. It was for a crippled world that
He came and died. At the outset of His earthly ministry He read from Isaiah and announced His mission,
to preach the gospel to the poor, to heal the broken-
hearted, to preach deliverance to the captives and re-
covering of sight to the blind, to set at liberty them
that are bruised, to preach the acceptable year of the
Lord. The Broken-hearted, the Bound, the Blind, the
Bruised—it is the same lame world at the Beautiful
Gate that He came to deliver. When John the Baptist
inquired from prison, "Art thou he that should come,
or do we look for another?" our Lord replied that He
was running on schedule: the blind were seeing, the
lame walking, the lepers were being cleansed, the deaf
were hearing, the dead were being raised, and the poor
were hearing the Gospel.

Has He ever ceased? According to the very first verse
of the Acts, the Gospel of Luke is an account of all that
Jesus *began* both to do and to teach. He is still at it.
The Book of Acts is not the Acts of the Apostles but
the Acts of Jesus. He is still ministering to the *lameness*
at the gate.

But He works today through us. Here Peter and
John are His agents. They said to the lame man, "Look
on us." "And he gave heed unto them, expecting to receive something of them." They called attention to
themselves as the representatives of Christ. Every
time we ring a church bell, every time the minister
stands in the pulpit, we are saying to the world, "Look
on us, we have something for you." God pity them if
we have nothing, if they be a hollow farce instead of a
holy force!

Peter said, "Silver and gold have I none; but such

as I have give I thee: in the name of Jesus Christ of Nazareth rise up and walk." Not money but miracles! Thomas Aquinas was being shown the glories of the Vatican. "No longer does the church say, 'Silver and gold have I none,' " said the Pope. "Neither can she say, 'Rise up and walk,' " replied Aquinas. The lame man looked, "expecting to receive something." Millions today never go to church. Thousands go and are disappointed. Like the man in the parable, we have nothing to set before them, no bread for our friends who have come to us in their journey. Suppose you are invited to dinner. The host sets the table, spreads the silver, seats the guests, returns thanks, but serves no food! That is a perfect description of many church services. We invite the lame world to "look on us," and they give heed, expecting to receive something, but we have nothing to give.

Peter and John did not disappoint this man. After the *look* came a *lift*. Peter took him by the right hand and lifted him up. I hasten to add that with the *lift* came *life*, "and immediately his feet and ankle bones received strength." We are all in the uplift business these days. The church is in it. But much of it drops the cripple right back into his misery and lameness and sin. I am not interested in the uplift business. I'm interested in the New Life business! A lot of our uplifting these days is mostly "soap" and "soup" but very little "salvation." Many churches that once had life now give only a lift. And it is being found out. This world needs more than a temporary lift such as it seeks from a cigarette or a drink. It needs life, a lift that lasts. There are churches where one might go for twenty-five years and never learn how to be saved. There is a momentary stimulus in a clever sermonette, like a shot in the arm. There may even be a temporary reformation. But our Lord told us of the house, empty, swept and garnished, where the demon returned with seven more evil spirits more wicked than himself. That is what happens when there is a lift without life.

Peter and John lifted in the name of Christ: "In the name of Jesus Christ of Nazareth rise up and walk." If they had merely lifted the lame man to drop him again he would have been more crippled than ever. Peter and John gave the credit to Another: "And his name through faith in his name hath made this man strong." There is no power in the name "Baptist" or "Methodist" or "Presbyterian." There is no power in the name of a famous preacher. There is no power in the name of your church, though it may be as big as the Pentagon. There is only one name with life in it. "In the name of Jesus Christ of Nazareth, rise up and walk." We sing "He Lifted Me," "Love Lifted Me." His is the lift that lasts, because there is life in it. "Thou shalt call his name Jesus: for he shall save his people from their sins." "He breaks the power of canceled sin, He sets the prisoner free." His name through faith in His name makes the cripple strong.

There was not only a *lift* in this story, there was a *leap*. "And he leaping up stood, and walked, and entered with them into the temple, walking and leaping and praising God." Sometimes I have stood in a very dignified Sunday morning service while the congregation sang rather unconsciously:

> Hear Him, ye deaf; His praise, ye dumb,
> Your loosened tongues employ;

Ye blind, behold your Saviour come;
And *leap,* ye lame, for joy.

I have wondered what would happen if some brother
took the admonition seriously and actually leaped. I
am sure there would be an exodus of scandalized saints.
I am not advocating rolling in the hay and foaming at
the mouth. I am just as afraid of that as you are. But if
we have no leap in our feet these days we should have
it in our hearts. We have lost the leap in our churches
today. Is it because we do not have the *life?*

They had the leap in Bible days. David danced before the ark. He wrote, "He maketh my feet as hind's
feet." So said Habakkuk. Little children leap for joy.
"But we have grown up." It doesn't seem so at a football game or a political rally. "But we must be dignified." Some dear souls think themselves dignified,
when, really, they are petrified.

We have lost our leap and it worries church leaders.
An Episcopal bishop calls for more "religious fanati-
cism." A Methodist bishop pleads for a return to "the
emotionalism that made Methodism famous." A Baptist leader speaks of another denomination that is
going places today because, for one reason, "they are
not afraid to shed tears." MacLaren speaks of those who
are always advocating sober standards of feeling in
matters of religion by which they mean what our Lord
described in far less polite language as being neither
cold nor hot but lukewarm. We need not go to extremes. The remedy for lethargy is not epilepsy. But if
the heart is full of life it will have a leap!

This shouting cripple stirred up quite a commotion.
He got the preachers into trouble. All Jerusalem was
in an uproar. Peter and John were forbidden to

preach. The church held a prayer-meeting that ended in an earthquake. And it was all because of a *lameness* that *looked* and a *life* that *lifted*—and when the *lame* looked and was lifted, he leaped. That sort of thing always shakes Jerusalem. What moves the hearts of men is not conventions and committee meetings and pink teas of the Uplift Club, but cripples who have looked and been lifted and who leap because they have life.

# 5

# *The Christ of Experience*

IN THE FIFTEENTH CHAPTER OF FIRST CORINTHIANS, THAT resurrection classic, Paul declares the Gospel. It was the Gospel which he preached, which they had believed, wherein they stood and whereby they were saved. He presents *The Christ of History,* "Christ died"; *The Christ of Doctrine,* "Christ died for our sins"; *The Christ of the Scriptures,* "According to the Scriptures."

Then he sets forth *The Christ of Experience.* First, *The Experience of Others*: Christ was seen after His resurrection by Cephas, by the twelve, by above five hundred, by James, and all the apostles. Finally, he declares *The Christ of His Own Experience*: "He was seen of me also."

It is possible to know Christ as a fact of history and doctrine and Scripture, as a fact in the experience of others, but not as a reality in one's own life. Our Lord Himself said that some would come to Him one day having prophesied and cast out demons and done many wonderful works in His Name only to hear Him say, "I never knew you."

Thank God for *The Christ of History*: Christ came, Christ lived, Christ taught, Christ died, Christ rose. That is the historic faith. A popular writer of some years ago said he would be a Christian even if it were proven that Jesus never lived. But most of us would find no satisfaction in a mere Christ of tradition, of imagination and fiction. There is a fad today for reading popular novels about Jesus the Galilean teacher, then trying to pull up oneself by the bootstraps to emulate His example, but the true believer rejoices in fact, not in fancy—the Christ of history.

Thank God for *The Christ of Doctrine*. Christ died for our sins and rose for our justification. But one may come as close to Him as doctrine and still miss Him. Jesus said to Martha, "I am the resurrection and the life." Martha believed in the resurrection as a doctrine, but Jesus would have her see, not a doctrine, but a Person. Much of our fundamentalism needs to move from the doctrinal to the personal and warm its heart in His love. The church at Ephesus was orthodox enough and went after false doctrine with a vengeance. Jesus commended their fidelity to the faith, but, for all that, they had left their first love. They were hot about the doctrinal but cold about the personal!

Thank God for *The Christ of the Scriptures*. How He warmed the hearts of the Emmaus disciples as He expounded to them in all the Scriptures the things concerning Himself! But He said, "Ye search the Scriptures. . . . *And ye will not come to me, that ye might have life*." One may come as close as the Scriptures and miss Him! The Scriptures indeed present Him, and faith comes by hearing and hearing by the Word of God. But Christ is also the key to the Scriptures. Studying the Bible without personal love for Him may be as dry as dust.

Thank God for *the Christ of other people's experi-*

*ence,* not only of Cephas and the twelve and the five hundred who saw Him after He rose, but also of the witnesses through the centuries who have not seen but yet have believed, and, though now they see Him not, yet believing, rejoice with joy unspeakable and full of glory.

But it is possible to know Christ as a fact in history and doctrine and the Scriptures and the experience of others and yet not be able to say, "He was seen *of me.*" It was said of Thomas Chalmers that he had "an original experience of Jesus Christ." Paul's desire was, "that I may know him." He wanted no second-hand, by-proxy faith, he couldn't live on the experience of Peter or of the twelve or the five hundred.

One thinks of Thomas as "more sinned against than sinning." He heard the experience of others: "We have seen the Lord." But he said, "Except I shall see . . ." He wanted an experience of his own. Our Lord said to him, "Blessed are they that have not seen *and yet* have believed." That's where you and I come in! And it reminds us of that other verse, "Whom having not seen, ye love; in whom, though now ye see him not, *yet believing,* ye rejoice with joy unspeakable and full of glory." We walk by faith, not by sight.

The early Christians had seen Jesus, but they did not live on memories. There came a day when they saw Him not, but they went on *believing.* Eye experience had given way to heart experience.

When Philip witnessed to Nathanael, he said, "We have found him of whom Moses in the law and the prophets did write." "We have found him"—that is experience. "Of whom Moses in the law and the prophets did write"—that is Scripture. Then he invited

Nathanael to know the Christ of Scripture and experience for himself: "Come and see."

Andrew said to Peter, "We have found the Messias." Philip said to Nathanael, "We have found him." The disciples said to Thomas, "We have seen the Lord." Some are saying that our greatest need today is more apologists to defend the truth and make a good case for the Christ of history, doctrine and the Scriptures. But we are awfully short on apostles who have seen the Lord and out of a warm heart know how to tell others.

We make a lot of other people's experience and often try to live on the momentum of the past. We commemorate Wesley and Finney and Moody, but, alas, we do not duplicate. Elisha did not ask, "Where is Elijah?" There is no use asking, "What would Moody do today?" We are not to go around like Saul, trying to resurrect dead Samuels. Nor need we ask, "Where are the days of Elijah?" Sighing for the good old days is wasted time. The Lord God of Elijah lives, and Jesus is a present reality. He is not a memory like the fragrance of faded roses. He lives today.

After we have presented the Christ of history, of doctrine, of the Scriptures, and of the experience of others, let us be sure that we can add, "And He was seen of me."

It takes time to know Christ intimately. He has no favorites, but He does have intimates. It is easier to read history, doctrine, the Scriptures, the experiences of others, than to cultivate a deep fellowship ourselves. The mood of the age is against it and does not lend itself to the pursuit of an original experience of Jesus Christ. In our churches we are out to win banners and **raise quotas, not to know God!**

We are busy these days with union and unification, trying to get the saints together, but what is needed is unity, and that we find only in heart-fellowship with Jesus Christ. Tuning one piano to another is a tedious procedure, but tune each to the pitch of the tuning fork, and when they are in tune with that they will be in tune with each other. Attuned to Christ we have harmony with each other.

In our text Paul is setting forth the Gospel, and, strictly speaking, the Gospel is not that Christ came, lived and taught, but that He died, was buried and rose again. One may believe that He came and lived and taught, but if he does not believe that Christ died for our sins and rose for our justification, he is still in his sins and his faith is vain. The death, burial and resurrection of Christ are facts of history, of doctrine and of Scripture. But they may also be facts of actual, personal experience: "We are buried with him by baptism into death: that like as Christ was raised up from the dead by the glory of the Father, even so we also should walk in newness of life." We may know Him *and the power of His resurrection*. It is not imagination or mere inspiration, it is identification!

There is an imitation Christianity that talks of the quest of the historic Christ. It says little of either doctrine or the Scriptures, for it has little use for either. It never faces the heart of the matter, that Christ came, not just to live and teach, but to die for our sins and rise for our justification. That is the Gospel! Paul said, "Woe is unto me, if I preach not the gospel," and he not only meant, "Woe is unto me if I do not preach it," but "Woe is unto me if I preach anything else!"

The Gospel is verifiable not only in history, doctrine, the Scriptures and the experience of others. You can prove it for yourself. You don't have to stop with the testimony of Andrew or Philip. "Come and see" for yourself, and you will say, like the Samaritans of old, "Now we believe, not because of thy sayings: for we have heard him ourselves, and know that this is indeed the Christ, the Saviour of the world."

# 6

# *When It Doesn't Make Sense*

*Perplexed, but not in despair.*

I GREW UP IN THE HORATIO ALGER DAYS, WHEN THE numerous stories of that prolific writer made standard fare for country schoolboys. Old-timers will recall those sink-or-swim, bound-to-rise thrillers. They were all cut from the same cloth and had just about the same outline: country boy goes to town; prevents a railroad wreck by flagging the train; gets job as messenger boy; rescues banker's daughter from bandits; gets job in bank; falls in love with the banker's daughter and marries her; comes through at the happy ending sitting on top of the world.

It made good reading in those days before the realists began to wallow so morbidly in insanity and suicide. But, of course, most lives do not roll along in story-book fashion. A few do, and we rejoice that their lines have been cast in such pleasant places. A few Christians seem to move through this world on an ever-ascending scale: health, success, happy family life, serene old age and a glorious exit. But with most of

**44**

us life does not follow the Alger pattern, and with many it goes exactly the other way, through disappointment, pain, grief, broken dreams, and often into sinister situations that simply do not make sense. These days we are listening to ever-increasing stories of tragedy and heartache, and no superficial pious moralizing will meet the need nor soothe the heart. There is no use denying it, there is much that doesn't make sense, and thousands of saints are not only perplexed but in despair.

Now, Paul was in perplexity but not in despair. He was not whistling his way through the graveyard, however, nor was he merely "smiling through" or, Micawber-like, looking for something to turn up. His way out was not by painting the clouds with sunshine, wearing rose-colored glasses and quoting lovely poems about "God's in His heaven—all's right with the world!"

I am constantly encountering dilemmas that don't make sense. I have a picture of myself standing with two other preachers taken only a few years ago. One was rudely snatched from earth in an automobile collision with a drunken driver. The drunken driver escaped, but the splendid young preacher was taken from a fruitful ministry and a fine wife and little children. The other preacher in the photo died later in his forties, just a few weeks before the birth of his only child, a son he had longed for through the years. I saw that little fellow recently and was struck again with the unexplainable mystery of what just doesn't seem to make sense. Even now I am tramping the woods with another fine youngster whose father died some years ago. When I think how much he loved that

boy but had to leave him, and wonder why I am en-
joying that little fellow instead, there looms again the
perplexity of those enigmas that just don't fit into any
of our patterns.

Of course men have wrestled with such puzzles from
the beginning. It was Job's perplexity. Habakkuk con-
tended with it and gave us his blessed "Although" and
"Yet." Micah surveyed a dismal day when godly men
had perished from the earth, while the wicked pros-
pered. He got through to God, and a man had better
do that or he will go crazy. John the Baptist sat in
prison and doubtless pondered why Jesus could work
all His miracles but leave His forerunner in jail.

The text finds Paul in straits, "put to it but not put
out." Some things are given us to know (Mt. 13:11) but
some things are not for us to know (Acts 1:7), and,
unfortunately, we fail to learn much we could know
by trying to find out what we cannot know. The little
boy who couldn't understand why God put so many
vitamins in spinach instead of putting them all in ice
cream was learning early that things just don't work
out as we would do them if we had the universe in
charge.

Some things just don't make sense, but we may be
perplexed yet not in despair. The way out is not by
explanation but by revelation. The Bible does not
give us explanation for some of these riddles, but it
does supply revelation.

To begin with, *because things do not make sense to
us does not mean that they don't make sense at all.*
Joseph told his brethren that they meant it for evil
when they sold him into Egypt but God meant it for
good. It didn't make sense to Joseph or to Jacob, who

said, "All these things are against me." But Jacob was mistaken, for all things cannot be against us if all things work together for good. We have often used the well-worn illustration of the hand-sewed bookmark. On the reverse side one sees only a meaningless tangle of loose thread-ends, but on the front side one reads "God Is Love." We are often on the wrong side of God's providences and the threads make no sense to us. But they make sense to Him who understands the end from the beginning. It is always foolish to assume that what we cannot understand cannot be understood at all.

Furthermore, *because some things do not make sense to us now does not mean that they never will make sense.* Many things that God does we know not now, but we shall know hereafter. One does not eat flour or sour milk or salt or soda. But when these are properly mixed and baked awhile they come out Southern biscuits. There are happenings and events that are very disturbing when we try to digest them by themselves. But God mixes them as part of His recipe, and when they come out of His oven in the light of eternity we find that they were part of the "all things" that "work together for good." We run into plenty of trouble trying to isolate certain experiences and understand them torn from their context. What mistakes have been made along that line with Scripture! We cannot detach this event or that from the whole pattern of our lives and make sense of it. It must be viewed in the light of eternity. Some day we'll understand.

But a still deeper consideration remains. There is a higher viewpoint from which *things which don't make sense to our ordinary reasoning can make sense to our spiritual understanding even now.* The highest lesson God wants to teach us is to "trust Him regardless." If everything made sense to our understanding we would need no faith. If everything worked out in story-book style we would become complacent and spoiled. God wants to bring us to a higher plane, where He Himself is our portion and reward, where we can sing,

> Now Thee alone I seek;
> Give what is best.

To do this, God allows things that don't make sense, that baffle and perplex our ordinary understanding. We may never be able to understand them here. But we can do one of several things about them. We grow bitter and resentful, sulk and grumble, and murmur, "Is the Lord among us or not?" We can grit our teeth and "tough it out" with a stiff-upper-lip stoicism. We can resign ourselves to the inevitable and go around with a martyr spirit. But there is a better way. We can accept it as one of the methods God uses to bring us to walk by faith and not by sight. While we still may not understand it with our heads, it makes sense to the higher understanding of our hearts. This is part of that wisdom which cometh down from above, and if we lack it we may ask of God, who gives liberally and upbraids not. It is not learned in schools, and often theologians miss it, while the simplest souls learn it. We have seen these unexplainable providences completely bowl over the wise and mighty, while lowly souls who had learned to sanctify themselves against tomorrow took them in faith's stride. They did not know *why* but they knew *whom* and trusted the matter with Him. It brought peace and blessing and so it "made sense" after all, the highest kind of sense, the sixth sense of the spirit.

When our Lord commanded the servants at the feast of Cana to fill the waterpots with water, I am sure that it didn't make sense. What they needed was wine, not water. But they filled the pots with water, and when it was served the governor of the feast did not understand, but we read that "the servants which drew the water knew." Humble souls who co-operate with the Lord even when things don't make sense have an understanding of which "governors" often know nothing.

> Whatsoe'r He bids you, do it:
> Though you may not understand,
> Yield to Him complete obedience,
> Then you'll see His mighty hand.
> Fill the waterpots with water;
> Fill them to the very brim.
> He will honor all your trusting,
> Leave the miracles to Him.
>
>                    Author Unknown.

# 7

# Some Needed Corrections

SOME YEARS AGO IT WAS PROPHESIED THAT THERE WOULD come a day when we would hear the preaching of "religion without the Holy Spirit, Christianity without Christ, forgiveness without repentance, salvation without regeneration and heaven without hell."

We have arrived. I would like to change some of these terms and suggest some points on which we seriously need to correct our thinking, our preaching and our living.

To begin with, there is the very common misplaced emphasis on *evangelism without revival.* In the South evangelistic meetings are frequently called "revivals" when often they are anything else but that. Evangelism is the proclamation of the Gospel with the purpose of winning the lost to Christ. Revival is a fresh work of the Holy Spirit among Christians to bring them to confession of sin, renewed dedication and loving zeal for service. God's order is the winning of the lost through believers who themselves have first been made right with God, as David illustrated by his prayer, "Restore unto me the joy of thy salvation; and uphold me with thy free spirit. Then will I teach transgressors thy ways; and sinners shall be converted unto thee." Many a so-called revival is only a drive for church members, which adds more unsaved sinners, starched and ironed but not washed, to a fellowship where even the true believers have not been aroused for years. Many an evangelistic campaign finds the evangelist preaching to non-believers who are not even present, while a congregation of comfortable Christians sit untouched in their sins and not interested enough to bring one sinner to hear the Gospel.

The church must first repent. God begins His work with His own people. Our Lord's last message to the churches was not the Great Commission but a call to repentance. The average church needs to restore the mourner's bench, and the first mourners should be the members. When God's people humble themselves and pray and seek God's face and turn from their wicked ways, God will send showers of blessing and a harvest of souls. It is better to wake up five hundred Christians than to convert five hundred sinners, for if five hundred Christians really wake up, they will win more than five hundred sinners.

Another weakness that needs to be corrected is the present-day accent on *conversion without repentance*. Do not misunderstand me here. I know that eternal life is the gift of God and that there is nothing meritorious in our tears.

> Could my zeal no respite know,
> Could my tears forever flow,
> All for sin could not atone;
> Thou must save, and Thou alone.

What I do mean is that we have made it easy for hundreds superficially to "accept Christ" without ever having faced sin and with no sense of need. We are healing slightly the hurt of this generation, trying to treat patients who do not even know they are sick. We used to sing "Amazing Grace" with a fervor that is sadly lacking nowadays because we knew the meaning of that line, " 'Twas grace that taught my heart *to fear*."

There is no fear of God before the eyes of men these days, and, consequently, they know not the joy of having those fears relieved. Is it any wonder, then, that grace does not appear as precious as it did the hour they first believed?

The Scriptures speak of those who hear the Word and anon with joy receive it but have no root in themselves, but endure for a while, but when tribulation or persecution arise because of the Word, by and by they are offended. We need to beware of conversions that begin too gaily. Conversion does indeed bring joy, but usually it begins with sorrow. Said the Guide in *Pilgrim's Progress:* "I care not at all for that profession that begins not with heaviness of mind. The first string that the musician usually touches is the base when he intends to put all in tune. God also plays upon this string first when He sets the soul in tune for Himself."

Alas, we have today a dry-eyed generation, pure in its own eyes but not washed from its filthiness. Sin has been minimized until it is nothing to cry about. Of course, we do not mean that every genuine conversion must be accompanied with great bitterness and tears, but we have gone to the other extreme, and men join churches with heads erect and wills unbroken, with stiff necks and proud looks and hard hearts, lugging their sins along. Neither before nor after such professions of faith is there any burden over the plague of one's heart. It all springs from the modern attitude toward sin and hell and judgment and our new version of the Christian life as a glorified good time.

Repentance is almost a lost note in our preaching and experience and the lack of it is filling churches with baptized sinners who have never felt the guilt of sin or the need of a Saviour.

In the third place, we are hearing much these days of *dedication without separation.* Men and women, young people in particular, are invited to present their bodies a living sacrifice, but little is said about the verse that follows that exhortation: "And be not conformed to this world: but be ye transformed by the renewing of your mind, that ye may prove what is that good, and acceptable, and perfect will of God."

Of course, there is a false and Pharisaic separation that renounces things but never self. A church full of such people would be remarkable: they would go to church, read the Bible, pray in public, give a tithe, be strict in conduct—and go to hell. Such separatists make much of not dancing, smoking, or going to the theater, but know nothing of real spirituality.

Yet there is a real separation from the world and the things of the world. If we love the world, the love of the Father is not in us. We are to turn to God from idols and we are to turn from vanities to the living God. The Scriptures are explicit that "whosoever will be a friend of the world is the enemy of God." If the latter part of the sixth chapter of Second Corinthians does not mean separation from the paganism of this age, what else can it possibly mean? We are to have no fellowship with the unfruitful works of darkness but rather are we to reprove them. I think it was Billy Sunday who used to say that a worldly Christian was an anomaly, although he didn't use that word. He said one might as well speak of a heavenly devil.

The Christian soldier is not to entangle himself with
the affairs of this life. We have lost our pilgrim character today. Negative preaching has been discouraged
and we have accentuated the positive, forgetting that
we are not only to put on the Lord Jesus Christ but also
to make no provision for the flesh to fulfil the lusts
thereof. The Lord knoweth them that are His, but
every one that nameth the Name of Christ should depart from iniquity. Much is said about visiting the
fatherless and widows in their affliction—and well we
may—but there is strange silence about keeping ourselves unspotted of the world.

We have poked plenty of fun at the doctrine of
separation for years. For fear of being Pharisees, many
have ended up worldlings. Others seem to enjoy seeing
how near the world they can live without being of it.
Our Lord made it plain that the world hated Him and
would hate us because we are not of the world but have
been chosen out of it. We are not true New Testament
Christians if we are acceptable to this age.

Again, we are seeing much today of *service without
the spirit*. There is an appalling ignorance of the Person and work of the Holy Spirit in our great church
bodies. Says Dr. Mullins:

It is a strange and very significant fact that Christians
for nearly two thousand years have so generally neglected
the New Testament teaching as to the Holy Spirit. The
creeds of Christendom have done scant justice to the
doctrine and some of the greatest of them have scarcely
done more than barely mention His office work. The
Philadelphia Confession of Faith used by so many Bap-
tists, and the New Hampshire Confession also quite generally used, are without separate articles on the Holy

Spirit, although both of them make reference to His work in connection with other doctrines. The Westminster Confession, the Presbyterian standard, is also lacking in any adequate setting forth of the work of the Holy Spirit. . . . The doctrine of the Holy Spirit is so interwoven and intertwined with the whole of the Old and New Testaments that it is one of the strangest oversights that Christians should have neglected it so long." From "Baptist Beliefs."

As a consequence of all this, we are witnessing a lot of church activity that reminds us of Samson shaking himself when he wist not that the Spirit of the Lord was departed from him.

It is not what is done *for* God that counts, but rather what is done *by* Him, the work of His Spirit through our yielded wills. Programs, propaganda, pep, personnel, these are not enough. There must be *power*. God's work must be done by God's people God's way.

Let me suggest one other inadequacy that needs to be corrected. With regard to our Lord's return, we emphasize *preparation without expectation*. Of course, all too generally nothing is said of His return at all. Bringing in the Kingdom is preached, but not *bringing back the King*. One wonders how many today *love his appearing* (II Tim. 4:8). The precious doctrine is like an unwanted stepchild, ignored as though it were beneath the dignity of some even to mention it.

Many who do sometimes speak of it would give the impression that readiness for His return is enough. But the New Testament Christians were not only ready, they were expectant. It is one thing to be ready for a visitor, another thing joyfully to anticipate his coming. When I did pastoral visiting, some of my flock were ready for my call but showed little evidence of eager expectancy.

This note of hilarious anticipation is a rare thing among us today. There is interest in Bible prophecy in some quarters, a delving into all the mysteries of Daniel and Revelation. That is important but that can exist without an expectant heart. Militant premillennialism is not enough.

The early believers were not looking for something to happen, they were looking for Someone to come. Looking for the train to arrive is one thing, but looking for someone we love to come on that train is another matter. I fail to find in all our vast religious activities, our plans and projects to build a better world, our complicated machinery with wheels within wheels —in all this I fail to find much of that simple warm-hearted longing for the personal return of our Lord. That He will come back suddenly and set things right is ridiculed in favor of the long-range program we have substituted. But the heart does not warm up to plans and programs, it warms up to a person. We are so in love with our arrangements that we do not love His appearing. If it be objected that such expectancy dulls evangelistic zeal and missionary enterprise, all that is necessary to refute that ridiculous charge is to call the roll of God-blessed evangelists and missionaries. And back of them stands the New Testament example. Those believers lived soberly, righteously and godly in this present world, but while they so lived, they were looking for that blessed hope and the glorious appearing of the great God and our Saviour Jesus Christ.

*Even so, come, Lord Jesus.*

# 8

# Hindering Spirits

OUR SAVIOUR HIMSELF COULD DO NO MIGHTY WORKS IN Nazareth because of the people's unbelief. Some of us are concerned these days over the ineffectiveness of so much of our religious activity. For all our churches, schools, conferences, campaigns, movements, where are the greater works our Lord promised that we should do? The mountain labors and brings forth a mouse. What is it that limits the Holy One of Israel? How have we grieved the Holy Spirit?

Evan Roberts used to say that there were three spirits in any meeting, God's Spirit, man's spirit, and the evil spirit. There was an evil spirit at Nazareth. I venture to name three evil spirits among us today, among even Bible Christians, that make our meetings mediocre when they could be miraculous.

There is the *fighting spirit*. Now, there is a fighting spirit that is fitting and proper. We are to endure hardness as good soldiers of Jesus Christ, fighting the good fight of faith with spiritual weapons, clad in the whole armor of God. We need an aroused holy indignation against the devil and all his works. Some of our churches are peaceful because they do not believe anything enough to contend for, and are too ignorant of, or too indifferent to, the things of God to get into a conflict.

I have heard of a soldier in the Civil War who was asked, "How many of the enemy did you account for?" "None," he replied, "but then I got as many of them as they did of me!" Too many soldiers of the Lord are just about as effective. They need a fighting spirit. But most of the saints are fighting each other these days. The greatest danger to the church is not from without but from within. Most of our conflict these days is not over doctrine and principles. It is over a Christmas tree, maybe, or the color of the new church carpet or who shall be the third vice-president of the Sons and Daughters of I Will Arise.

When our Lord was on earth "there was a division of the people because of him." There always is such a division for he is the Great Divider. But most of our fusses and divisions come under another verse: "Mark them which cause divisions . . . and avoid them" (Rom. 16:17). We like to justify our pugnacity by calling it zeal for the truth, but we generally fight over personalities, not principles.

The Scriptures warn constantly against biting and devouring one another, against wars and fightings, against schisms and strife and clamor and bitterness and debates and contentions and swellings and tumults. Almost every suitable word in the vocabulary is used to describe sins of the fighting spirit. It leads to numberless isms and schisms, cliques and clans, super-separationism to the nth degree. Pity the man who tries to shepherd a flock of malcontents who mistake love of a fight for love of the truth!

And what shall we say of the way we fight back when

we are wronged? If the Bible teaches anything it certainly sets before us a Saviour who, when He was reviled, reviled not again; Christians who took joyfully the spoiling of their goods, and constant advice to be patient under persecution. But how often we hear Bible Christians publicly express bitterness over wrongs, either fancied or real? What becomes of leaving vengeance to the Lord? Are we not told to take wrong and even suffer ourselves to be defrauded?

Any Christian has only to read his New Testament to see how grievous to the Spirit of God are these manifestations of the *fighting spirit*. What seething resentment and hidden anger lie buried beneath the pious faces of a lot of fundamentalists! We would be a picnic for any psychiatrist. While we declaim on the need and causes of revival, we could get a lot nearer to such an awakening if we confessed our gripes and grouches and became reconciled to our brethren.

Again, our Saviour cannot do many mighty works among us because of a *frivolous spirit*. We are in favor of good humor and have been accused sometimes of using it too freely. There are those who imagine that to be all out for God they must look "all in." We are to beware of hypocrites of a sad countenance appearing to fast. But it is very easy to cross over from humor to levity, to foolish talking and jesting. "Good fellowship" among God's people is a precious thing, and God does not expect us to talk about spiritual matters all the time we are engaging in such fellowship. But there is an inherent seriousness in our message and mission and our manner should befit both. Besides, the days are evil, the time is short, and we are in the midst of a world emergency which requires that our conduct should match the crisis. The men of God in the Scriptures do not suggest the present-day back-slapping, uproarious variety of sanctified morons cracking jokes sometimes doubtful, and making puns on sacred Scripture.

For all this we shall doubtless only bring another laugh from this superficial generation. But the mood of the age is one of frivolity and not a few have fancied that the cause of Christ can best be advanced by being jolly good fellows after the pattern of this world. It is true that the Pharisees probably had no sense of humor, and we are familiar with their raised eyebrows at the joyous message and behavior of the Saviour and His disciples. But neither can we imagine the Man of Sorrows in the rôle of whooper-upper, nor "see" Peter and Paul making clowns of themselves to attract a generation of buffoons.

There is no evidence that the church has had any influence on Hollywood, but there is plenty to prove that Hollywood has influenced the church. It is impossible for human nature to accept the philosophy of the first two chapters of First Corinthians, and Christians themselves simply can't get over the notion that we help the Gospel along by aping the fashion of this age, appealing to its culture, its tastes and fashions. God never meant that His revelation, which is, and always will be, foolishness to them that perish, should be revamped and streamlined to make it acceptable to the natural man. Men must square with the Gospel to be saved, must see themselves lost, repent and be born again. To cater to their pride and tickle their ears in order to make them favorably disposed to hear our message is to defeat the purpose of the Gospel.

We have all failed along this line and would do well to check up on our frivolity. What starts out as innocent fun grows rapidly and easily runs away with the best of us. It is not easy to draw the line, but it were better to err on the side of seriousness. Happy Christians are indeed a testimony but what the world calls happiness is not what God calls joy. The natural man has no appreciation for the joy of the Lord any more than he has for anything else of grace, and will never have any taste for it until he is converted. Christians' brand of happiness is not his, and when we act funny to try to impress him that one can be a Christian and have a good time we generally succeed only in making ourselves ridiculous and belittling the cause we represent. We forget that the life in Christ springs from an entirely different source and runs counter to this age from beginning to end.

The Scriptures are not geared to frivolity, and the tone of the Gospel, while it is indeed Good News, is Good News of a feast, not a frolic. No great revival ever started in fun-making nor ran on such fuel. There is joy aplenty, but it is the heavenly joy of the Spirit of God and not the silly antics of human clowning under religious auspices.

Another spirit that hinders the work of our Lord today I would call, for lack of a better term, the *fed-up spirit*. His own words, "Woe unto you that are full," could be applied today to a surfeited generation stuffed with carnal satisfactions, having exhausted all the thrills and sensations that the world, the flesh and the devil can offer. But I am thinking just now of an entirely different application. While millions have never heard the Gospel and while multitudes even in our own land are pagans, with no knowledge of the Truth, we have the strange spectacle of thousands of Christians who have heard so much and read so much that they have reached the saturation point. Stuffed with Bible knowledge, they have become spiritual dyspeptics, rich and increased with goods and having need of nothing.

"The ill of all ills is the lack of desire," says Faber. When I was a boy I heard only two sermons a month. Good preaching was scarce in those parts, and we appreciated a real sermon. But the years have passed and now it is easy to hear sound preaching in our Bible conferences and churches and by radio. But when the rare becomes commonplace, familiarity may breed contempt or at least smug indifference. Children who have too many toys soon thrill to none. I can remember how rare a thing ice cream was in the boyhood days on the farm. A sundae or a soda was an event. Now they are common, but I am sure I do not enjoy them as once I did. I wonder if something like this has not happened to us Christians with regard to Divine truth. There was a day when I had never heard a great Gospel singer. I remember the tremendous thrill when I listened to Charlie Alexander for the first time and heard Charlie Butler move a great convention. The years have passed and I have heard the best in singing and in preaching, and now I fear that I may join those who have become full. I am afraid that precious truths that ought to stir us and bring tears to our eyes and hallelujahs to our lips now leave us cold. We sit like spiritual connoisseurs, glorified critics, inwardly sizing up what we hear, putting the truth into mental cubbyholes. This we give to the Jew and that to the Gentile and the other to the Church of God and receive none of it ourselves. We compare preacher with preacher, classify him in our private catalogue, and go out discussing Paul, Cephas, and Apollos.

There was a time in my life when I knew nothing of many precious truths taught in our sound churches and schools and conferences today. I remember the day when I first tasted of these things and reveled in such blessed draughts for my thirst. But for years I have lived day by day in the midst of this feast, have read and heard and taught these glorious teachings, and I am sure that my greatest peril is satiety. The edge of our appetite becomes dulled. What once almost made us leap in the aisle now almost puts us to sleep in the pew.

I do not think any evil spirit hinders our Lord more than this. Do not forget, you who so lightly regard these stupendous truths you have heard so much, you who can sit half-asleep and yawn at what once made men gladly face prisons and torture and death—do not forget that there are multitudes in total darkness who if they could hear a little of what you hear so much would shout for joy to know that God so loved the world that He gave His only begotten Son.

I have preached to various types of congregations. I have ministered to listeners in some of our churches who are what we call worldly: they know next to nothing of the Bible; they may smoke or play bridge or go to the movies. I have preached to others who were outright sinners, making no profession to know Christ. I find it easier any day to awaken these people than to arouse to action smug saints comfortably reposing in

their orthodoxy, neither cold nor hot and having need
of nothing.

The *fed-up spirit* is a deadly spirit, and all the more
dangerous because those most infected with it are least
responsive to any challenge about it. We have become
wise and prudent but God has revealed His secrets to
babes. I am not pleading for gullibility. There is much
error abroad and we must try the spirits, but we easily
overdo things and sometimes sit with our guard up
when we might relax and become receptive. We must
remember that it is the age of the racketeer, religious
as well as otherwise, and somebody is forever trying to
peddle something at our elbow or over the air, until
we have built up an unconscious resistance to any form
of persuasion. But if we believers do not somehow
manage to become humble and childlike and receptive
and rejoice and weep together in our meetings instead
of sitting like a flock of stenographers collecting epi-
grams for our notebooks, we are going to turn out to
be the driest generation of saints in all church history.

You will observe that I have spoken to myself as well
as to you. I think I can say that I am conscious of these
perils and concerned about them. There is hope for a
gracious awakening among us if we will honestly face
up to these hindering spirits and see what hold they
have on us. It was unbelief that hindered our Lord at
Nazareth. Wherever humble souls simply believed,
He always worked His miracles. Religious Pharisees,
taught in Scriptures, separated from the world, stood
critically by and missed the blessing, while the plainest
of people felt the power of God. If we can renounce our
childishness and sit at His feet in childlikeness, He
will do His mighty works again.

# 9

# *God's Cure for Ignorance*

*But as the days of Noe were, so shall also the coming of the Son of man be. For as in the days that were before the flood they were eating and drinking, marrying and giving in marriage, until the day that Noe entered into the ark, and knew not until the flood came, and took them all away; so shall also the coming of the Son of man be.*

MATTHEW 24:37–39.

SEVERAL TIMES IN THE NEW TESTAMENT (ROM. 11:25; I Cor. 10:1, 12:1; II Cor. 1:8; I Thess. 4:13; II Peter 3:8) we read, with slight variations, "I would not have you ignorant."

I am sure that the people of Noah's day must have been amused at this strange preacher who built an ark while he warned his generation of impending judgment. Today it would be a popular diversion to drive out on Sunday afternoons to watch this eccentric prophet build his oversized houseboat. But just the same, Noah was right and his contemporaries were wrong. They may have been intelligent and progressive but they were ignorant of God's program. *They knew not.*

Our Lord says that in the last days men will be just like that. Life will be a matter of "eating and drinking, marrying and giving in marriage, buying and selling,

planting and building." As it was in the days of Noah
and Lot, so shall it be, said our Lord, and so it is today.
The milling throngs on our crowded avenues do not
know which way the wind is blowing, they do not
know what time it is, they do not know what the score
is. *They know not.*

Josh Billings used to say, "I'd rather know a few
things fer certain than be sure of a lot of things that
ain't so." It may offend some of the higher-ups, but the
outstanding characteristic of this generation is ignorance. And yet there never has been a generation that
prided itself more on its cleverness, smartness, and
sophistication. We are the "most-read," not the best-
read, people in history. We never had more college stu-
dents and never more ignorance, not only outside our
schools but inside, because there is such a thing as edu-
cated ignorance. A leading American educator said,
"The intelligence of the race has failed before the
problems which the race has raised."

We never had so much smartness and stupidity at
the same time. We know a lot about a lot of things, but
of God's Word and will we are of all men most ignorant. And whatever else a man may know, if he does
not know what God wants him to know, he is an igno-
ramus. Our Lord said, "Ye do err, not knowing the
scriptures, nor the power of God." When we are ignorant of these things, we live in error. We travel faster
today than ever. John Wesley lived centuries later than
Julius Cæsar, but he could travel no faster. But what
avails our speed if we are going in the wrong direction?
In the last hundred years we have learned many interesting things about the world we live in, but we have
not learned any better how to live in it. We correct one

social evil, and a dozen more break out. We conquer one disease, and a new one takes its place. We build schools and churches on almost every other block, but our jails fill with young gangsters, and churches are deserted by a mad generation loving pleasures rather than God. Dress modern man in the latest attire, give him a college diploma, put him in a limousine with every new gadget attached, start him on an American highway, but, if he is left to himself, he is as dumb as a sheep; he wanders in a wilderness of error, and ends up in eternal hell.

The people of Noah's day *knew not,* and we know not. We are ignorant, we know not the Scriptures or the power of God. We know the baseball scores, but we cannot read God's scoreboard. The people of Noah's day scoffed at him, and Peter tells us that in the last days scoffers shall arise. He goes on to say, "For this they *willingly are ignorant of,"* that Noah's world was destroyed by water and ours will be destroyed by fire. Some people are ignorant because they want to be.

You will remember that, at the outset of Paul's voyage to Rome, he warned that there would be trouble. The captain of the ship advised otherwise. They listened to the captain of the ship and sailed away to shipwreck. Today men listen to the captain of the ship, to the expert instead of the prophet and— behold the consequences! Like Ahaziah, we consult Baal as though there were no God in Israel. And, true to form, the experts have landed us in that "perplexity" which our Lord said would be a mark of the last days—the state of one who has lost his way.

About the time of World War I, something snapped in America. Something went out of us that has never come back. Until then we were more or less old-fashioned. Progress had not run us crazy. We still had time to live. The old virtues were still preached and practised. It was still the custom for husbands and wives to live together. We still believed the Bible—at least we respected it. Then the world went crazy and we have been in a madhouse ever since. A new climate environed us. Evolution boasted that we were on our way from protoplasm to Paradise. Higher criticism denied the Scriptures, minimized sin, reasoned away the atonement, air-conditioned hell. Man was deified and God was humanized. Liberalism dismissed the devil, and now when we have more devil than ever, though we never had fewer people who believe there is a devil. Although modernism threw him out the door, neo-orthodoxy now tries to get him back through the window. Anyway, we decided we were able in ourselves to achieve our salvation. We started on a spree and have been reeling ever since.

*They knew not.* Paul speaks in Ephesians of the Gentiles "alienated from the life of God through the *ignorance* that is in them." Peter says we are not to fashion ourselves according to the former lusts in our *ignorance.* By well-doing we are to put to silence the *ignorance* of foolish men. Paul says Israel was *ignorant* of God's righteousness, and he told the Athenians of the unknown god "whom ye *ignorantly* worship."

Who is ignorant? The man who does not know God's Word and will. Who is wise? The man who does know God's Word and will. Some who do know are well-educated, with as many degrees after their names as have been devised. But they did not learn it that way. They had to become fools to be wise. The wisdom of

God is foolishness to men and is learned only in the school of Christ. The natural man can never know the Scriptures or the power of God.

We need not be ignorant. We can know whom we have believed. We can know we have passed from death unto life. We can know He abides in us by His Spirit. We can know that all things work together for good to us who believe. God has said repeatedly, "I would not have you ignorant." He would not have us ignorant concerning spiritual gifts (I Cor. 12:1), concerning them which are asleep (I Thess. 4:13), concerning God's purpose with Israel (Rom. 11:25), concerning God's measurement of time (II Peter 3:8). Paul says "we are not *ignorant* of Satan's devices." Certainly we should not be, but many of us are.

The answer to ignorance is Christ Himself, who is made unto us wisdom, for He is the Truth and Wisdom of God. A college student said, "Education gives me spokes for my wheel but no hub." Jesus Christ is the Hub, by Him all things consist. That is why a janitor sweeping the steps of a library, if he knows Christ, knows more than a philosopher inside who knows not Christ. Head-knowledge is useful, but unless it is sanctified by the Holy Spirit it can be the most dangerous thing in the world. Germany had knowledge, but she wrecked our world. Hitler knew his program but not God's. At first he seemed to succeed. His war machine rolled over Poland and Norway and France and the Balkans and into Russia. But Hitler tackled one race of which it was said by God Himself, "I will bless them that bless thee, and curse him that curseth thee" (Gen. 12:3). When he tried to exterminate the Jew he ran into God's program, and no man can interfere with God's program and win.

I have heard of a spider that tried to build its web on the moving hands of a town clock. Just as futile is the plan of any man to build against God's plan of the ages or God's will for his life.

The only man who can understand the times is the man who views them in the light of the Living and the Written Word. Suppose, on a starry night, I found you on a hilltop viewing the heavens. Suppose I suggested to you, "Friend, I have a telescope which you may use," and you replied, "Oh, no, why should I limit myself to that tube when I have two good eyes and can look everywhere unhampered?" But you could see more in a moment by confining your view through the telescope than you could behold all night with your unaided vision. Just so do the wiseacres today scoff at restricting themselves to the Bible viewpoint. As well might a minnow complain at confining itself to the Atlantic Ocean!

No man with God's telescope need ask, "What are we coming to?" He knows. We are not of the night but of the day. We are not to be unwise but understanding what the will of the Lord is. We are to walk circumspectly, not as fools but as the wise, buying up the opportunities because the days are evil.

God expects us to understand His program and get in step with it. He is not converting the world nor saving civilization. It has been said that Pentecost did not save Jerusalem from falling to the Roman armies, but saved people out of Jerusalem; that, on his voyage to Rome, Paul was not concerned with saving the ship but with saving the passengers. God is taking out a people for His Name. Christ is the Great Gatherer, and he that gathereth not with Him scattereth abroad. We are not out to salvage a wreck but to save people out of the wreck.

Henry Ward Beecher once said of D. L. Moody, "He is a believer in the second advent of Christ and in our own time. He thinks it is no use to attempt to work for this world. In his opinion, it is blasted, a wreck bound to sink—and the only thing worth doing is to get as many of the crew off as we can and let her go. I should be a burning fire all the time if I believed like that, though I do not say I must believe like that to be a burning fire."

Well, Moody was like Noah and he was right. We live in a generation that knows not. Let us stand on God's sure Word, God's cure for ignorance. Then our hearts will be fixed, trusting in the Lord, not disturbed by evil tidings. For "great peace have they which love thy law: and nothing shall offend them."

# 10

# Gilgal to Gilboa

NEXT TO JUDAS ISCARIOT, THERE IS NO MORE TRAGIC figure in all the Scriptures than Saul, King of Israel. No man ever got off to a better start. And no man ever had a sadder finish.

Saul was tall and good-looking, which is not to be despised. Once in a while—not often—God makes a handsome man, just to relieve the monotony. Saul had gifts of leadership, for there followed him a band of men whose hearts the Lord had touched. On occasion, he could use good sense. While his critics scoffed, he held his peace. Blessed is the man who can restrain himself when the children of Belial revile him. He was reticent at proper times, as when his uncle asked him what Samuel had said. Some of us tell all we know —and more.

Yet Saul was a tragic failure. He had his good moments and mastered a good many situations, but he never mastered himself. His days ended in the weird setting of a spiritist séance followed by suicide on dark Gilboa. All the way through his career from Gilgal to Gilboa various incidents showed him up, but they were only symptoms of a malady that lay deeper. He was impatient, could not wait on Samuel but offered the sacrifice himself. When Samuel appeared—he had a habit, like Elijah, of showing up at most embarrassing moments—Saul tried to explain instead of repenting. He displayed a violent temper toward Jonathan and jealousy because of David's success.

But the episode that really furnishes the key to his trouble has to do with the slaughter of the Amalekites. God commanded the utter extermination of both people and possessions. Saul spared their king, Agag, with the best of the sheep and oxen. Once again Samuel appeared right at the critical moment. It was a dramatic meeting, loaded with significance. Saul started on a high key: "Blessed art thou of the Lord: I have performed the commandment of the Lord."

Just then a sheep bleated or an ox lowed. And Samuel bluntly demanded, "What meaneth then this bleating of the sheep in mine ears, and the lowing of the oxen which I hear?" Something always happens to betray the man who professes to be what he is not. He may maintain that everything goes well, but one day there will be the telltale bleating of the sheep. The worst thing about our sins is not that they will be found out but that they will find us out, show us up, at some awkward moment. Here God used a lowly ox to confound a king, and no matter how well we think we have concealed the matter, somewhere in our life of disobedience the sheep we should have slaughtered will bleat at the most inopportune moment and show up the farce our pious chatter cannot hide. Saul's procession included things God had told him to destroy. The man who insists on lugging along idols and affections and wedges of gold and sheep and oxen God has commanded him to exterminate will stand confused by those very accursed things on some day of judgment.

The worst of it is that when Saul was caught up with, he did not humble himself and repent. True, he said, "I have sinned," but he brought forth no fruits meet for repentance. It is a mark of the unyielded self to argue the case, to try to explain, to justify oneself. Saul tried to explain that the sheep and oxen had been spared to sacrifice unto God at Gilgal. But the end did not justify the means. Money made the wrong way is not sanctified by giving God a tip out of it on Sunday morning. God will not accept an offering of the fruits of disobedience.

Samuel's immortal answer clears that up forever: "Hath the Lord as great delight in burnt offerings and sacrifices, as in obeying the voice of the Lord? Behold, to obey is better than sacrifice, and to hearken than the fat of rams." One may give up worldly amusements, give his goods to feed the poor, give God time and talent, and never obey God at the heart of the matter by giving himself. The Macedonians first gave *themselves* to the Lord. Our Saviour said, "If any man will come after me, let him deny *himself* . . ." The trouble with Saul was that he never gave up Saul.

But Samuel went deeper in his immortal answer and analyzed Saul's trouble with one word: "For rebellion is as the sin of witchcraft, and *stubbornness* is as iniquity and idolatry." We do not classify stubbornness with iniquity and idolatry, but God does! He says, "I will instruct thee and teach thee in the way which thou shalt go: I will guide thee with mine eye. *Be ye not as the horse, or as the mule,* which have no understanding: whose mouth must be held in with bit and bridle, lest they come near unto thee" (Ps. 32:8, 9). We are frequently compared to various animals in the Scriptures, and some of the comparisons are not very complimentary! God wanted to instruct Saul in the way he should go and guide him with His eye, but Saul was as stubborn as a mule. Someone has said that a mule is always backward about going forward. Certainly Saul would not be guided by the will of God.

He said, "I feared the people and obeyed their voice." Samuel had just spoken of "obeying the voice of the Lord." Samuel was the voice of the Lord, but Saul obeyed the voice of the people. We have an old adage, *Vox populi, vox Dei* ("The voice of the people is the voice of God"), but it isn't the voice of God. The man who listens to *vox pop* is doomed from the start.

Saul pretended to be sorry, but only to keep the support of Samuel. He begged the prophet not to leave him, but the chapter ends with the king rejected of God and hastening on to ruin. A few pages farther we come to the sad finish. We read that Samuel was dead, and, try as he would, Saul could get no answer from God. In desperation, he turns to a spiritist medium, the very thing he had outlawed earlier. Put it down as a sure mark of the man who fights the will of God, he will turn back to something he once ruled out. I have seen it done again and again.

Here we have the story of a king trying to call back his lost opportunity. Saul had his Samuel. David had his Nathan. Ahab had his Elijah. Herod had his John the Baptist. Blessed is the man who listens to his prophet and heeds his oracle. Most of us have had a Samuel, maybe a good pastor, godly parents, a faithful wife, a loyal friend, someone through whom God would help us toward a better life. Thank God for them, but God pity the man who treats his Samuel as Saul treated his! Men trifle with those voices, and there comes a day when Samuel no longer warns us and we are left to our doom. And how many miserable Sauls today would like to call back a presence departed and hear a voice now still!

When Nathan faced David with his sin, you remember, the king repented, and in the immortal Fifty-first Psalm cried to God, "Thou desirest not sacrifice; else would I give it: thou delightest not in burnt offering. *The sacrifices of God are a broken spirit: a broken and a contrite heart, O God, thou wilt not despise.*" Where Saul failed through stubbornness, David won through submission.

God uses broken things. It takes broken soil to produce a crop, broken clouds to give rain, broken grain to give bread, broken bread to give strength. It is the broken alabaster box that sheds forth perfume. It is Jacob limping from Jabbok who has power with God and men. It is Peter weeping bitterly who returns to greater power than ever.

We hear that stubborn wills need only redirection, but God says they must be broken. A little boy whose mother made him sit still said, "I may be sitting down, but I'm standing up inside!" What a lot of inner rebellion is hidden under external religion these days!

Sin is having one's own way instead of accepting God's way. "We have turned every one to *his* own way." The sinner is not asked to give his heart to God. God gives him a new heart, then says, "Son, give me thy heart." We have a generation of unbroken Sauls on our hands today. They grow up stubborn in the home and are disobedient to parents. They go to schools where the natural man is glorified. They never learn to say, "I'm sorry," to man, and it is not surprising that they will not say it to God. It is deemed a mark of weakness. So they make their stubborn way—personality must not be thwarted but grow uninhibited and unhampered!

Stubbornness breaks more hearts, wrecks more homes, divides more churches, fills more hospital beds and suicides' graves than any other form of iniquity, for the root of most troubles is an unbroken self.

In the New Testament there was another man named Saul. Once he was just as stubborn as the Old Testament king. But one day God met him on the Damascus road, knocked him down, broke him up, and made him over, and named him Paul. The Old Testament Saul started with a crown and ended under a cross of his own making. The New Testament Saul submitted to a cross, was "crucified with Christ," and ended with a crown of Glory. Both were headstrong fellows, but one took the path of stubbornness to suicide, while the other chose the way of submission and became the greatest preacher of all time.

The Gilboa Road and the Damascus Road! The tendency today, even in many pulpits, is to invite young Sauls to become Christians without any repentance, any breaking down before the Lord, any crucifixion with Christ, any unconditional surrender to the will of God. They join our churches with heads erect and wills unbroken, with stiff necks and proud looks and hard hearts. So we have thousands of church members lugging their sins along, unsanctified flesh pretending to serve God, the old Adam parading under religious auspices. It is Saul and not Paul. The mourner's bench may have been misleading sometimes, but it was better than proud sinners walking down church aisles pure in their own eyes and yet not washed of their filthiness. Young people gaily "accept Christ" and with joy receive the Word, but afterward show no evidence of a new heart. We are trying to produce blessedness without any preceding bitterness, rejoicing without repentance, making the house of God a delightsome place before it has ever been a dreadful place where repentant sinners meet God.

God help our young Sauls today! Part of the blame is on us that we have failed as Samuels. We have humored their headstrong stubbornness and failed to declare that God demands the sacrifice of a broken heart. They will learn it, but for many it will be too late. Let us try to save them at Gilgal lest they come to Gilboa.

# 11

# Back to the Spring!

I HAVE HEARD SOMEWHERE OF A SPRING WHOSE WATERS had certain medicinal properties so that those who drank from it were helped in the case of various infirmities. In the course of time, homes sprang up around the spring, then a hotel, stores, and eventually, a town that grew into a city. But there came a day when visitors would ask, "By the way, where is the spring from which this grew?" and dwellers in the city would rub their hands in embarrassment and say, "I am sorry that I cannot tell you, but, somehow, in the midst of all our progress and improvement we lost the spring and no one knows now where it is."

There is a sad application here for the church. Under all our ecclesiastical superstructure today we have lost the spring. We have been lost on the circumference and need to get back to the Center. We are out on the periphery and must needs find the Person by whom all things consist. We are majoring on the minor and minoring on the major. We need to relocate the Spring.

Paul stayed at the Spring, he never left the Center. There was plenty of sin in the New Testament days, but the early Christians did not busy themselves organizing anti-slavery societies and anti-Rome clubs. They gloried in Christ.

Jesus Christ is the issue. He always made Himself the issue. "He that is not with me is against me; and he that gathereth not with me scattereth abroad." It is Christ or AntiChrist. Theoretically, we all agree to that. Ask any comfortable Sunday morning congregation and they will nod approval. But it is not as simple as it looks. Break up that congregation into individuals and you will get a different story. Some are more interested in being vice-president of a club or circle than in all-out loyalty to Jesus Christ. They are interested in projects and preachers and movements, but their primary devotion is not to Jesus Christ. If He Himself were supreme our hearts and homes and churches would not be as they now are.

Our sole business is to glorify Jesus Christ. Someone has said, "There is only one thing in which God is interested and that is the exaltation and glorification of His Son. He is not interested in glorifying any individual, group movement, or body of people, or ecclesiastical system apart from Christ. He is interested in these only to the extent they exalt and glorify His Christ."

We agree to this theoretically, but actually our loyalty is to men and movements and systems, however loudly we may protest that such is not the case. Paul did not say, "To me to live is Christ first." He said, "To me to live is Christ." Christ was everything, first and last, Alpha and Omega.

The Christian experience may be set forth in four F's: Faith in Christ, Fellowship with Christ, Faithfulness to Christ, and Fruitfulness for Christ. Certainly it begins with Faith in Christ. "Believe on the Lord Jesus Christ and thou shalt be saved." "I know whom I have believed." Everything else grows out of relationship with Christ and identification with Him. Think of the thousands who are depending on church or creed or character to save them. Thousands of church members have never been saved. We are trying to win to fellowship with Christ and faithfulness to Him many who need first to come to faith in Him. We beg backsliders to dig up musty church letters from the bottoms of trunks, join the church and go to work, with the idea that it will straighten them out spiritually. But we have reversed God's order. A man in proper relationship and fellowship with the Lord will be both faithful and fruitful all along the line, self, service, substance; but to reverse the procedure will not bring him into proper relationship and fellowship. These grow out of identification with Christ, they do not produce it. Joining church, attending church, tithing, and all the rest of it will follow getting right with Christ.

"He that is not with me is against me"—there is position, relationship, identification: "He that gathereth not with me scattereth abroad"—there is practise, faithfulness, fruitfulness. "Lovest thou me? Feed my sheep"; "He that abideth in me and I in him, the same bringeth forth much fruit"—there is the proper order.

Americans are notorious joiners. Give them a red button and a certificate and they will join anything. But joining a church does not join them to Christ. We must begin with that personal faith in Him by which we become members of His body.

We need to get relocated these days. To use the story

with which we began, we need to find the spring somewhere among the skyscrapers we have built over it.
Every great revival has begun with someone rediscover-
ing the spring. The Quakers, Moravians, and Methodists began with someone finding the spring. But, like
Ephesus, we get away from it. The great campaigns of
Moody, Torrey, Chapman, Gypsy Smith and Billy Sunday brought the saints together around the spring
again. Now and then in church history the city becomes
too big, the ecclesiastical superstructure too complicated, and God starts out another man looking for the
spring—faith in and fellowship with the living Christ.

Dr. Torrey used to give as the first step toward a revival: "Let a few members of any church get thoroughly right with God." Lenin said, "It is better to
have a hundred fanatics than a thousand placid followers." The children of this world are wiser on this point
than the children of light. Let a nucleus of real Christians thoroughly right with God start from Center,
start from the spring, and expand, winning lukewarm
Christians into fellowship and unsaved sinners into
relationship with the Living Christ.

In geometry we use a compass with one prong sta-
tionary while we describe our circle with the other.
Christ is the fixed center: "All power is given unto
me"; our circumference is the world: "Go ye into all
the world." And if we do not expand, the world, the
flesh, and the devil will contract. If we do not push
out, the devil will push in!

It is too late in the day for many of our vast projects
and programs. There is time just to be Christians and
to win others to be Christians. The issue is Jesus Christ,

faith in and fellowship with the Living Christ that issues in faithfulness and fruitfulness.

Let us check ourselves on the four F's. Let us exam-
ine ourselves whether we be in the faith. How about
*faith in Christ?* Do we really believe, trusting Him with
living faith to the saving of the soul?

What about *fellowship with Christ?* Is our fellowship with the Father and with His Son Jesus Christ?
(I John 1:3). Is it the fellowship of the Spirit? (Phil.
2:1). Is it fellowship in the Gospel? (Phil. 1:5). Are we
walking in the light so that we have fellowship one
with another? (I John 1:7). Do we know anything
about the fellowship of His sufferings? (Phil. 3:10).
Do we have fellowship with the unfruitful works of
darkness? (Eph. 5:11). There can be no heavenly fellowship if there is a hindering fellowship.

Along with *fellowship with Christ* goes *faithfulness
to Christ.* "It is required in stewards that a man be
found faithful" (I Cor. 4:2). Mind you, it is not op-
tional, take-it-or-leave-it; it is required. We have been
espoused to one husband and married to Christ, and
unfaithfulness is adultery. John wrote to Gaius, "Thou
doest *faithfully* whatsoever thou doest." Do we work
faithfully or is it flashily or fitfully? Shall we merit one
day the final commendation, "Well done, thou good
and faithful servant"?

If we are in fellowship and faithful, we shall be *fruitful.* We are married to Another, even to Him who is
raised from the dead that we should bring forth fruit
unto God (Rom. 7:4). If we abide in Him we shall
bring forth much fruit. There is the *fruit of the spirit,*
love, joy, peace, long-suffering, gentleness, goodness,

faith, meekness, temperance (Gal. 5:22, 23). Pity the Christian who claims to be living in the land of Canaan, with its figs and pomegranates, if all he has to show is crab apples!

We are to be fruitful unto every good work (Col. 1: 10). We are created in Christ Jesus unto good works. But good works will not create us in Christ Jesus. Going to church, singing in the choir, giving our tithe, witnessing for Christ, these issue from faith and fellowship. "Lovest thou me? Feed my sheep"—that is the order.

There is another kind of fruit often overlooked. The fruit of marriage is children, and we may have children in the faith. Paul spoke of Timothy as his son. He spoke of Onesimus as one begotten in his bonds. To the Corinthians he wrote, "In Christ Jesus I have begotten you through the gospel." One may be a spiritual father to the souls he wins to Christ. And a grandfather to many more! Think of the man who won Moody to the Saviour!

Faith in Christ, Fellowship with Christ, Faithfulness to Christ, Fruitfulness for Christ—here is the heart of the matter. In the midst of building the city let us take time out to relocate the spring!

# 12

# God's "Inevitable Progress"

FOR SOME YEARS BEFORE THE BOTTOM FELL OUT OF
civilization we heard much about the inevitability of
progress. The evolutionists with all their kith and kin
assured us that man was as sure to move forward as the
sparks to fly upward. We have not heard much of that
lately. The only inevitability now mentioned is that
of world destruction, at least the possibility of the extermination of the human race.

With the wiseacres now looking for a hole in the
ground in which to escape from their own inventions,
it is very evident that if we are progressing it is in reverse. Instead of creating a millennium we have con-
trived a madhouse.

But there is one kind of progress that is sure. The
eternal purpose of God moves on. God's program is
running on schedule. He will arrive where He is going.
Let us consider three ways in which the growth of
God's purpose is revealed. *The God-Man grew on.*
*God's men grow on. God's message grows on.*

First, *The God-Man grew on.* Almost two thousand
years ago God solved the greatest problem of all time,
how to be a just God and yet justify ungodly men. How
can a holy God and unholy men be brought together?
Something had to be done about the sin problem.

85

There was nothing that man could do. But God so loved the world that He gave His only begotten Son. When we were without strength, in due time Christ died for the ungodly. There had to be someone who was both God and man to bring together God and men. God solved that problem by sending His Son, who had no sin in Him but took all sin on Him, was made sin for us though He knew no sin, that we might be made the righteousness of God in Him.

So He came, born of a woman, and was laid in a manger in Bethlehem. Of course, the devil was not asleep. He got busy immediately to try to destroy the God-Man. King Herod was his instrument. All the children two years old and under in that part of the country were slain. But Joseph and Mary, warned of God, fled with the baby Jesus to Egypt. There they stayed until Herod died and the angel advised Joseph to return, "for," said he, "they are dead which sought the young child's life." They always die who run against the purposes of God!

Then we read that the child Jesus was taken to Nazareth, and Luke tells us: *And the child grew and waxed strong in spirit, filled with wisdom: and the grace of God was upon him; and Jesus increased in wisdom and stature, and in favor with God and man.* The God-Man grew on and grew up, died and rose again, and accomplished our redemption. God's purpose prevailed, the devil was defeated, Herod died. But *The God-Man grew on.* Little did proud Rome know, little did cultured Greece imagine, little did religious Israel suspect, little did poor Nazareth dream, that in that little village, working at a carpenter's bench, was the Son of God and Son of man. Even a worthy Israelite

asked, "Can there any good thing come out of Nazareth?" Indeed, all that is good came out of Nazareth,
for in Him dwelt all the fulness of the Godhead bodily.

In the second place, *God's men grow on.* In the Old
Testament we read of the boy Samuel whose mother
gave him to the Lord even before his birth. After he
came she took him up to Eli the priest at Shiloh, and
there he grew up. It was an evil age. Eli was old and
his sons were immoral and the nation was backslidden.
The calamity howlers and viewers-with-alarm, no
doubt, were lamenting that the good old days were
gone forever. But amidst all the sin and shame, the im-
purity and the infidelity, we read, *And the child Samuel grew on, and was in favor both with the Lord, and
also with men,* reminding us of the similar verse about
the child Jesus. God had His eye on that boy, for His
eyes run to and fro throughout the whole earth, waiting to show Himself strong in behalf of those whose
heart is perfect toward Him. Then came the night
when God called and Samuel answered, and we read
after that, *And Samuel grew, and the Lord was with
him, and did let none of his words fall to the ground.*
Thus began a glorious career as the last of the judges,
counselor of kings, and spokesman for God. *God's man
Samuel grew on.*

In the New Testament there is a similar statement.
It was another evil day. For years there had been no
prophet in Israel, and the fire of the Spirit had died
low. God's people lived under a heathen power and
religion and had sunk into dead formalism. But God
sent to earth another boy to grow up outdoors and be
the forerunner of the God-Man Himself. We read of
John the Baptist that *The child grew, and waxed*

*strong in spirit, and was in the deserts till the day of his shewing unto Israel.* God's man John the Baptist grew on!

So it has been through the centuries. There has never been a time so dark and dismal and desolate but somewhere God had a boy growing on. Remember that the days were dreary and the outlook desperate while the boy Martin Luther grew on. And the boy John Wesley, and the boy George Whitefield, and the boy George Fox, and the boy Charles Haddon Spurgeon, and the boy Dwight L. Moody. If you had seen any of these at the age when God called Samuel, you might not have suspected that here was God's man growing on. In Wales a lad in the coal mines prayed for years that God might endue him with the Spirit for revival. God heard him, for Evan Roberts was God's man growing on to spark the great Welsh awakening.

One thinks of the feeding of the five thousand. Here is an emergency, a multitude hungry and without food. But there are no unforeseen emergencies with God. Andrew reports, *"There is a lad here* which hath five barley loaves and two small fishes." Ah, God has a boy on the spot! Of course, Philip took a dark view of the possibilities: "But what are they among so many?" But when this boy gave to Jesus such as he had, and all he had, the miracle happened.

Preaching is such a thrilling business. When my eye runs over the congregation and I see boys scattered here and there, I take heart. There may be a Samuel growing up among them! There may be a John the Baptist down there getting ready to be a voice in the wilderness. Never mind if he is not brilliant or prepossessing. He may have but loaves and fishes, but "lit-

tle is much if God is in it," and that light lunch blessed
and broken and distributed by the Lord will feed a
multitude. Never take your congregation lightly,
though it be small and unimpressive; one of God's men
may be growing up in it.

What a challenge to every parent who has a child in
the home! He may be God's man growing on. Give him
every needed counsel and correction, teach him to listen when God speaks. No man or woman ever had a
nobler challenge or a higher privilege than to bring
up a child for God, and whenever we slight that privilege or neglect that ministry for anything else, we live
to mourn it in heartache and grief. There were many
things that my father did not have, but one thing he
did have: he had a consuming ambition that in his
home a boy should grow up to live for God.

God's men grow on but God expects some assistance
from us in helping them to grow on.

> An old man going on a lone highway
> Came in the evening cold and grey
> To a chasm yawning both deep and wide.
> The old man crossed in the twilight dim;
> That swollen stream was naught to him.
> But he stopped when safe on the other side
> And built a bridge to span the tide.
> "Old man," said a fellow traveler near,
> "You are wasting your time in labor here;
> Your journey will end with the closing day,
> You never again will pass this way.
> You've crossed the chasm deep and wide.
> Why build you this bridge at eventide?
> The laborer lifted his old grey head:
> "Good friend, in the way I have come," he said,
> "There followeth after me today
> A youth whose feet must pass this way.

This chasm which has been naught to me
To that fair youth may a pitfall be.
He too must cross in the twilight dim;
Good friend, I am building this bridge for him."

                              Author Unknown.

Yes, *God's men grow on,* and blessed is he who has a part in their progress.

Finally, I would have you observe that *God's message grows on.* We have already seen how one King Herod tried to destroy the child Jesus, but, instead, died himself while the *God-Man* grew on. Years later, another Herod tried to stop the progress of the early church by killing James and putting Peter in prison. A little later, we read that "the angel of the Lord smote him . . . and he was eaten of worms, and gave up the ghost," and then, in striking contrast, it is declared, *"But the word of God grew and multiplied."* Herods rise and fall, but God's message grows on. The kings of the earth set themselves and the rulers take counsel together against the Lord and against His anointed, but what happens? The worms get them, not only in body but also in soul, where the worm dieth not and the fire is not quenched. And under the epitaph of every enemy of the Gospel we may add, *"But the word of God grew and multiplied."*

When the power of God fell on Ephesus under the ministry of Paul, we read that fear fell on them all, and the name of the Lord Jesus was magnified; that many believed and confessed and burned their evil books, and again there follows the comment, *"So mightily grew the word of God and prevailed."* The very essence of a spiritual awakening is this, that *God's message grows on.*

Here is a progress that is really inevitable. "For as the rain cometh down, and the snow from heaven, and returneth not thither, but watereth the earth, and maketh it bring forth and bud, that it may give seed to the sower, and bread to the eater; *so shall my word be* that goeth forth out of my mouth: it shall not return unto me void, but it shall accomplish that which I please, and it shall prosper in the thing whereto I sent it." There may be setbacks and temporary defeats. God's message may seem to lose some battles but it will not lose the war!

Someone stood on an ocean beach and observed the incoming tide. Wave after wave broke on the sands, but the tide came in on schedule! Out of that experience grew a blessed illustration of how God's message always wins:

On the far reef the breakers recoil in shattered foam;
Yet still the sea behind them urges its forces home;
Its chant of triumph surges through all the thunderous din,
*The wave may break in failure but the tide is sure to win.*

O mighty sea, thy message in changing spray is cast:
Within God's plan of progress it matters not at last,
How wide the shores of evil, how strong the reefs of sin;
*The wave may be defeated but the tide is sure to win.*

Author Unknown.

Amid all the wreckage of civilization today one thing stands eternally certain: the purpose of God will prevail. We see not yet all things put under Him, but we see Jesus. The God-Man, God's men, and God's message are bound to win. Some may object by saying that there are more heathen now than ever, that there is more sin than ever, that the world is farther from be-

ing converted than ever. That is just another proof of
the truth of our proposition. God's Word never said
the world would be converted but that perilous, not
prosperous, times shall come in the last days, that evil
men will wax worse and worse, that because lawlessness
shall abound, the love of most will wax cold. And it
declares that just as the God-Man Christ Jesus came on
time when first He came in grace, so He will come on
time when He comes again in glory.

I would warn you, however, on one point. Just because God's plan and purpose are sure to win does not
mean that you are to sit idly by and watch it win. God
works His plan by working His people. The God-Man
finished His work as our Saviour, but the proclamation
of that finished work is not finished. God's men grow
on, but we can help them grow on in a thousand ways.
God's message grows on, but it grows as we go to take
it and to send it.

It is a dark hour and the only light today is provided
by the God-Man, who said, "I am the light of the
world"; by God's men, of whom He said, "Ye are the
light of the world"; and by God's message, of which it
is said, "The entrance of thy words giveth light." We
are to *see the light* when we look unto Jesus in saving
faith. We are to *be a light,* for He told us to let our
light shine before men; and we are to *send the light* to
the people in darkness, for how shall they hear without
a preacher and how shall they preach except they be
sent?

Here is the unbeatable combination, God's winning
team; the God-Man, God's men, and God's message.
Here is the only inevitable progress. Here is the one
growing movement that will not die. Long ago the

enemies of the Gospel were baffled even then because they could not stop it: prison doors would not stay shut, nor would the mouths of Gospel preachers. We read that the puzzled rulers *doubted . . . whereunto this would grow*. Well, it is still growing and if we do not grow with it we die. Make sure that you are born into it and that as it grows you grow in grace and in the knowledge of our Lord and Saviour Jesus Christ.

# 13

# From Ruin to Redemption

"I FEEL LIKE A WRECK!" SO GOES THE COMMON EXPRESsion nowadays, and well it may. We live in a day of wreckage. Some of the world's great cities have been ruined. Our highways are marked by wrecks caused so often by "the nut at the steering wheel." Our hospitals are filled with mental and physical wrecks. Up and down our streets walk thousands more who still manage to get around.

For all the ruin, most of us are afraid that the worst is yet to come. Badly in need of repair as we are, we are fearful, what with atomic power at our command, that we are in for more damage than ever.

The fact is, we are all wrecks and we have been living in a wreck all the time. It must have been a lovely earth when Adam had dominion. It is still beautiful in spots, though now marred and broken. There was a day when man ruled the earth, when there was no bloodshed, nothing to hurt or destroy. But Satan came and Adam sinned and nature came under the curse. We lost our dominion and we have never regained it. We cannot whistle and have the birds obey us or crook the finger and make the fishes come at our bidding. We have lost our dominion and must snare the animals and go forth armed to meet the worst of them, lest we fare like the big game hunter I read about recently of whom somebody said, "It is feared that something he disagreed with ate him."

The loveliest scene of nature is deceptive because underneath there is bloodshed and terror; the creatures creep about in fear, the birds look nervously in all directions, the snake crawls in the grass. Everything is under the curse, just a wreck of its original glory.

But there is coming a day when nature will be at peace. The lion and the lamb shall lie down together —and the lamb will not be inside the lion! The first Adam failed, but two thousand years ago there came a second Adam. He had dominion, and there are signs of it all through His days on earth. He stilled the tempest, healed the sick, turned water into wine, raised the dead. He knew just where a certain fish could be caught, rode an unbroken colt into Jerusalem, and had a certain little rooster all set to crow at just the proper time on the night of Peter's denial. He did not use His dominion as fully as He could have when He was here the first time, but one day He will return to reign over a redeemed earth, and then it will not be a wreck. But it is a wreck now, and the whole creation groans in expectation of that day of redemption.

A desert traveler was awakened in the night by a strange unearthly sound sweeping across the wastes, something between a sob and a sigh. He awoke the old guide, who explained, "Ah, it is the desert crying." Immediately there flashed on the traveler's mind those words from Romans: "For we know that the whole creation groaneth and travaileth in pain together until now. And not only they, but ourselves also, which

have the first-fruits of the Spirit, even we ourselves
groan within ourselves, waiting for the adoption, to
wit, the redemption of our body."

I am something of a bird-lover. I used to tramp the
woods somewhat saddened at times, because, no matter
how lovely the day, how sweet the bird songs, how fra-
grant the flowers, there were everywhere present the
evidences of pain and death and decay, the marks of
the bondage of corruption. It was a great day when
there dawned on me that blessed truth, so neglected
and unknown, that it will not always be so:

> The wolf also shall dwell with the lamb, and the leopard
> shall lie down with the kid; and the calf and the young
> lion and the fatling together; and a little child shall lead
> them. And the cow and the bear shall feed; their young
> ones shall lie down together: and the lion shall eat straw
> like the ox. And the sucking child shall play on the hole
> of the asp, and the weaned child shall put his hand on the
> cockatrice' den. They shall not hurt nor destroy in all my
> holy mountain: for the earth shall be full of the knowledge
> of the Lord, as the waters cover the sea  (Isa. II:6–9).

Not only is the earth a wreck, but civilization is a
ruin. Civilization is not going to the dogs, it is headed
for the vultures. With a most loathsome figure, our
Lord described the final state of man before His coming: "Wheresoever the body is, thither will the eagles
[vultures] be gathered together" (Lk. 17:37). For all
our vaunted science and boasted inventive genius, we
are now mainly occupied with trying to find means of
escape from the results of our inventions. A popular
book bears the title, *No Hiding Place*. A leading sci-
entist writes on the subject, "I'm a Frightened Man."
A recent cartoon pictures a cave man at his cave en-

trance greeting a modern citizen trying to find refuge from atom bombs. The greeting is, "Welcome home, brother!" Civilization is a wreck, and our progress will end in ruin.

Civilization is a failure because the human race is a failure. "By one man sin entered into the world and death by sin"; "All have sinned"; "In Adam all die." Just as nature's loveliest landscape is deceptive, so is all our effort to make earth's wreck look like the Garden of Eden. I sat in a little Southern city on a beautiful morning looking across the placid surface of a tranquil lake. It was one of those rare days in June when, if ever, come perfect days, when earth seems in perfect tune and all nature in accord. But my peaceful meditation was jarred when I perceived that the waters reflected a hospital that stood on the other side. That spoke of sickness and pain and death. No matter how we dress up our cities and beautify our dwelling places, we must have hospitals and morgues and police stations, all the paraphernalia of a ruined race.

But two thousand years ago there came to earth One who said, "My kingdom is not of this world." He stood condemned on that occasion, and it appeared that He had failed. But it was haughty Pilate who failed. The old Adam has failed, but the second Adam came down in all the wreckage of our race and became the firstborn of a new race. And as many as receive Him, to them God gives the power to become the sons of God. There is a new commonwealth of those whose citizenship is in heaven, pilgrims and strangers looking for a city. One of these days there will be the manifestation of these sons of God. We are coming into our own! Every knee will bow and every tongue confess that Jesus

Christ is Lord. One thing I am sure of, there is coming a day when every skeptic will agree with me and every unbeliever admit that my message is true, but it will be too late for them. I can afford to wait but they cannot. If you are sitting in the seat of the scornful it is high time to get into the new race by the new birth, and move out of ruin into redemption.

Individually, we are all wrecks. We were ruined by the fall, the curse of Adam's sin is on our bodies and minds. No matter how husky or attractive you may be, you started to die the day you were born, and every day you have one day less to live. You may not yet be aware of disintegration, but you soon will be! Some of you realize it well already. Maybe your eyes have failed. Maybe right now you are wearing out your neck trying to get used to bifocals and have discovered that no eyes are like the ones God gave you. Perhaps your teeth have failed, and "the voice of the grinding is low," and you may be reading this with your new teeth in your pocket! We are disintegrating because our present outfit, both physical and mental, is in the bondage of corruption.

Our minds are wrecks, and, therefore, we make so many mistakes. We are just a shell of what we were in Adam, for sin and Satan have done their work. We are headed for the grave. We may get drunk and forget it, live in pleasure and make light of it, but

> The boast of heraldry, the pomp of power,
> And all that beauty, all that wealth e'er gave,
> Awaits alike the inevitable hour.
> The paths of glory lead but to the grave.

It is a good thing to "forefancy your deathbed," as an old saint put it. The modern emphasis on "Get ready to live, not ready to die," sounds very up-to-date, but no man is more ready to live than the man who is ready to die.

Does this sound like pessimism? I have not finished yet! The best is yet to come. Two thousand years ago our Lord came, not only to give us a foretaste of the day when nature shall be reclaimed, not only to begin the new race of the sons of God, but to die for our sins and rise again to guarantee that those who live in Him shall have new bodies and live forever with Him. Our salvation is free, but not yet full in our actual experience. Recently a preacher suggested that we use the word "salvage" instead of "salvation." But we merely salvage the same old wreck, while salvation guarantees us a new outfit. I don't want to be towed into heaven behind a wrecking crew; I want to go in brand new!

The best is yet to come. "To die is gain," and being a Christian makes death a paying proposition. That blessed assurance that Jesus is mine is but a *foretaste* of glory divine. We that have the first-fruits of the Spirit groan within ourselves waiting for our new bodies. "The earnest expectation of the creature waiteth for the manifestation of the sons of God."

It is true that we are merely shells of what we were in Adam; but we are also but shadows of what we shall be in the Second Adam. I am not what I was, but neither am I what I shall be. "Beloved, now are we the sons of God, and it doth not yet appear what we shall be: but we know that when he shall appear, we shall be like him; for we shall see him as he is." Every time I look into a mirror I am well aware that it doth not yet appear what I shall be!

I am not now what once I was,
Nor am I what I want to be;
But what I am I am by grace,
And when I see Him face to face
I shall be like Him perfectly.
I once was dead yet thought I lived;
And now I live, yet dead I am;
I live in Him with whom I died;
I to the world am crucified,
My life, my song, is Calvary's Lamb.

Author Unknown.

These blessed truths hold for us both an encouragement and a warning. For one thing, while it is true that we are wrecks and the resurrection is still ahead, there is a very real sense in which the Spirit strengthens our bodies and minds here and now, to enable us to do His will. We are identified with Christ and are members of His body, and as we live by simple faith and obedience in complete dependence on Him, the power of God in Christ flows in and through us, empowering us to do all God wants done. Some go to extremes here and expect too much in the present body, thinking they should have no pain and make no mistakes. Others go to the other extreme, struggling along in their own strength, living on their reserves instead of on His resources. He is able to make all grace to abound so that we may abound. But we must come to the end of our reserves, that extremity which is God's opportunity. The woman who touched Jesus had come to the end of her reserves, physically and financially. The rich young ruler still had reserves of his own, so he went away without the blessing.

Paul was a wreck. He had a thorn in the flesh. I

# FACTS
# You Should Know
# And Believe
# TO BE SAVED

By
M. G. B.

He that believeth not is condemned already, because he hath not believed in the name of the only begotten Son of God. — John 3:18.

It is appointed unto men once to die, but after this the judgment. — Hebrews 9:27.

But—

He that heareth My Word and believeth on Him (God) that sent Me (Jesus) shall not come into judgment. — John 5:24.

For God sent not His Son into the world to condemn the world; but that the world through Him might be saved. — John 3:17.

Being convinced that I am a sinner, and knowing that "Christ died for my sins, and that God hath raised Him from the dead", I now want to confess Jesus as my Lord before men.

SIGNED

think his eyesight was bad. They said his bodily presence was weak and his speech poor. But he could do all things through Christ—that is, all things that God wanted him to do. There is provision even for our present bodies and minds to enable us to do His will.

But there is a fearful warning here. It is bad enough to live in the wreck of a body in the wreck of a race in the wreck of a world. But if we do not avail ourselves of the new life in Christ we are doomed to the eternal wreckage and garbage heap of hell, where the worm dieth not and the fire is not quenched. Whosoever does not believe shall *perish*.

What a prospect, however, awaits the child of God! "For we know that if our earthly house of this tabernacle be dissolved, we have a building of God, an house not made with hands, eternal in the heavens." The apostle goes on to say that we groan while we live in this tent, desiring to be clothed upon with our house from heaven. In Romans he tells us that the whole creation groans and that we groan, but the Spirit helps our infirmities, interceding for us with groanings which cannot be uttered.

A little boy sitting in the door of a mountain cabin was asked, "Do you live here?" "Yes," he answered, "but we've a new house up on the hill and we're moving tomorrow. You can see farther, the water's better, and everything's brand-new." If your tent is fast deteriorating, brother, we're moving up higher soon. You can see farther, the water is better, and everything will be brand-new.

> Some day the silver cord will break,
> And I no more as now shall sing;

But O the joy when I awake
Within the palace of the King!

Some day my earthly house will fall
I cannot tell how soon 'twill be;
But this I know, my All in All
Has now a place in heaven for me.

Some day: till then I'll watch and wait,
My lamp all trimmed and bright;
That when my Saviour opens the gate,
My soul to Him may take its flight.

From "Some Day The Silver Cord
Will Break," by Fanny Crosby.

# 14

# *Christ's Call to Revival*

*Repent . . . or else . . .—*

REVELATION 2:5, 16.

PERHAPS NOTHING IS MORE CLUTTERED WITH FALSE NO-
tions and contradictory ideas than the matter of revival. More energy has been misdirected, more carts
put before the horse on this theme than on almost any
other that engages our attention. A revival is not an
evangelistic campaign. It is not a church paying out
of debt or erecting a new building or putting on a
stewardship campaign. These things may flow from a
revival, but they do not constitute one. A revival is not
a drive for church members.

A revival is a work of God's Spirit among His own
people. David prayed, "Restore unto me the joy of
thy salvation; and uphold me with thy free spirit. Then
will I teach transgressors thy ways; and sinners shall
be converted unto thee." That is God's order, and He
has never changed it. A lot of so-called joy of the Lord
is merely whipped-up emotion which leaves a lot of
unconfessed sin and hidden iniquity. We have made
convalescents of church members who need operations. We have tried to cure them with sunshine, leaving the focal infection untouched. Nathan did not tell

David to play on his harp. He made David see himself
to be a sinner and ready to pray, "Create within me a
clean heart."

Dr. G. Campbell Morgan divides his treatment of
First Corinthians into two parts. He tells us that Paul
dealt first with the carnalities, then with the spirituali-
ties. Today we ignore sin in the midst and pass over the
carnalities on the popular argument that we should
never be negative but deal only with the positive. But
there are churches that have accentuated the positive
for years, while the members have lived among the
negatives. Men will not desire a physician until they
know they are sick, and they will not seek a closer walk
with God so long as they are content to get along without it.

There is, however, a wrong emphasis in preaching
on revival. Sometimes it has created the impression
that revival is a spurt of religious enthusiasm which
it is not possible to live up to the year round. As a
matter of fact, what we call revival is simply New
Testament Christianity, the saints getting back to
normal.

Most Christians have been subnormal so long that
when they become normal they are thought to be ab-
normal! A boy and girl had danced all night in a road-
house. Early in the morning they walked out of the
dance hall reeking with the smell of whisky, beer, and
tobacco. Outdoors, the girl suddenly sniffed and said,
"What is that I smell?" "That's not a smell," the boy
replied. "That's fresh air!" We have lived so long in
the swamps of a low-grade Christianity that the fresh
air of the hills stuns us when it strikes us.

Many revival sermons are preached from Old Testament texts: from Second Chronicles seven, verses thirteen and fourteen, the revivals under Hezekiah or Ezra, or other portions. But one does not have to stay in the Old Testament to preach on revival. A preacher suggested to me some time ago that there was nothing about revival in the New Testament. Certainly there is not much about it in the Acts. They didn't need a revival; they had a "vival"; and there was no need of reviving. But as one moves on through the book, he finds such words as, "It is high time to awake out of sleep," or "Stir up the gift of God that is within you." Perhaps the supreme call to revival is from the lips of our Lord Himself in the Book of Revelation. The last word of our Lord to the church is not the Great Commission. The Great Commission is our marching orders; the last word of Christ to the church is, "Repent." To five out of seven churches in Asia it was His message. Many churches today are not ready to carry out the Great Commission until first they repent.

In some quarters we hear much of the Christ of the Gospels. There is a place for that, for He is not only our Saviour but our Example, and in the Gospels we see how He walked. We hear much of the Crucified and Risen Christ, and there we have the Gospel. We hear of the Coming Christ, and there we have our Hope and a mighty incentive to revival, for he that hath this hope purifieth himself, and that is the essence of revival. His return is not a lullaby to put us to sleep but a reveille to wake us up! But we need also a vision of the Glorified Christ among the candlesticks, with His eyes as fire, His feet as brass, and His voice as the sound of many waters; with seven stars in His right hand, a two-edged sword proceeding from His mouth, and His countenance as the sun in its strength. The greatest preacher of revival is the Glorified Christ of Revelation.

The church needs to face Christ. He is the Issue; we must settle with Him. There is a lot of soft, sentimental talk about Him today that brings no conviction. When Isaiah saw the Lord, he did not feel comfortable! Neither did Habakkuk nor Daniel nor Paul nor John. We want a picture of Him today that does not disturb us, that smiles at sin, and winks at iniquity. I remember a man who told me he wanted to hear no hell-fire sermons but rather about the meek and lowly Jesus. Yet the poor man did not seem to realize that the meek and lowly Jesus said more about hell than is reported from the lips of anyone else in the Bible! We need a true and complete vision of God in His holiness and Christ in His glory that will bring us to repentance.

The great awakenings of the past have been accompanied by preaching against sin, and for conviction, repentance, godly sorrow, confession and forsaking of sin, restitution, return to first works, return to the Scriptures, and prayer and witnessing and godly living. We are willing to do anything but repent. In our great church gatherings you cannot get many "Amens" on a call to repentance. Of course, there are polite references to it occasionally, but real repentance that would put us all on our faces from the top officials on down would be awfully humiliating. Besides, we haven't time for a revival, for our programs are all set up, and if God wants to send a revival He must do it in the week allotted to it; any other time it would upset the schedule.

Our Lord's message to the churches was, and is, "Repent—or else." It is revival or removal. Ephesus was *loveless,* orthodox—busy—but loveless. Are we not guilty today? Jesus said, "By this shall all men know that ye are my disciples, if ye have love one to another." What is the badge of discipleship? Stately buildings? Stained-glass windows? Robed choirs? Impressive statistics? It was love! Tertullian writes that it was said of the early Christians, "How those Christians love each other!" Today the world might sometimes be more inclined to say, "How those Christians hate each other!" We have left our love for Christ, and when love for Christ dies, love for each other, for the Bible, for souls, dies.

Again, the church at Sardis was *lifeless.* It had a name to be alive, mind you, but the Lord pronounced it dead. Our Lord does not always have the same name for us that we have for ourselves!

Laodicea was *lukewarm.* A little too hot to be cold and a little too cold to be hot, and don't forget that the Lord did not say He would spew them out for being too hot! He would even prefer that a man be on the wrong side of the fence than *on* the fence.

But His message ends with a positive note: "Behold, I stand at the door and knock." We apply that to sinners, but it was spoken to the church, a self-sufficient church, with Christ on the outside. "If *any man* open the door . . ." One man can start a revival. Someone has said that Christ is waiting, not for a committee to pass a resolution, but for one man to let Him in. Laodicea had everything but Jesus.

He comes in as guest and abides as host. "I will come in and sup with him and he with me." At Cana, and with the Emmaus disciples, He was first the guest, then the host. Alas, in our homes we put Him in a picture on the wall, but too often He is not the Head of the house. In our churches we may put Him in stained-glass windows but never let Him in the door. Back of all else, we may carry His Name on our lips but never crown Him in the throne-room of our hearts. The way to revival, in heart, home or church, is to open the door to Jesus.

# 15

# *Catacombs and Colosseums*

A RECENT MAGAZINE ARTICLE CARRIES A PICTURE OF THE ancient Colosseum of Rome and speaks of it as the place "where early Christians died for a faith *the world now takes for granted*."

The writer, perhaps, spoke more truth than he meant to say. However much we take our faith for granted now, it certainly was not a matter of course in the heyday of the Colosseum. That Flavian amphitheater, still a show-place in modern Rome, was built by Jewish slaves. The outside walls cost more than fifty million dollars. It seated no less than fifty thousand people. In its arenas gladiators and wild beasts fought for public entertainment. One thousand animals were slain there on an emperor's birthday.

If we had sat in those grandstands amidst "the grandeur that was Rome" we might have been deceived. For it was not the howling mob in the Colosseum that determined the course of history. Underground in the catacombs another force was working. A handful of men and women who worshiped another King called Jesus, who had died and risen and was coming back some day—here was the beginning of an empire within an empire, the Christians beneath the Cæsars. They crept along the subterranean passageways and tunnels, among the tombs and caverns, hunted and persecuted, "the scum of the earth." If we had prowled around in these gloomy depths we might have come on little companies singing, listening to a Gospel message, observing the Lord's Supper. We might have said, "They haven't a chance." But the Christians underground eventually upset the Cæsars above ground. The catacombs overcame the Colosseum and finally put the amphitheater out of business.

There is something fascinating about these saints of the catacombs. It has intrigued our writers and showed up in *Quo Vadis* years ago, and in similar books today. We cannot forget this fellowship of simple believers who loved Jesus Christ more than their lives, in the world but not of it, whose blood was the seed of the church. It was said of them long ago: "They live, each in his native land but as though they were not really at home there. They share in all duties like citizens and suffer all hardships like strangers. Every foreign land is for them a fatherland and every fatherland a foreign land. They dwell on earth but are citizens of heaven. They obey the laws that men make, but their lives are better than the laws. They love all men, but are persecuted by all."

These denizens of God's Underground were on fire with a passion which swords could not kill nor water drown nor fire destroy. Their blood was spilled so freely in the arena that a traveler was asked, "Do you want a relic? Take a handful of sand from the Colosseum. It is all martyrs!"

Here was a minority group in a pagan land, but, like many minority groups before and after, they changed the course of history. Today the professing church has grown rich and increased with goods and needs nothing. As the magazine writer said, the faith is now taken for granted. What once was asserted is now assumed. We sing,

> Our fathers, chained in prisons dark,
> Were still in heart and conscience free:
> How sweet would be their children's fate,
> If they, like them, could die for Thee!

But we are a pretty comfortable crowd of Christians, who seem to forget that for us the Gospel is not something to come to church to hear, but something to go from church to tell. The cause of Christ is not carried forward by complacent Sunday morning bench-warmers who come in to sit but never go out to serve.

The worst of it is, we have moved from the arena into the grandstand, from the catacombs into the Colosseum.

Certainly we have caught the *spirit* of the Colosseum. One would think Christians had never heard those Scriptures, "But not conformed to this world"; "Whosoever therefore will be a friend of the world is the enemy of God"; "If any man love the world, the love of the Father is not in him." The gods of Rome—the lust of the flesh, the lust of the eyes, and the pride of life—are still our gods, and we "fear the Lord and serve our own gods."

Campbell Morgan said we Christians are not to catch the spirit of the age but to condemn it, and, so far as we may, correct it. But churches are filled with worldlings. They sit in the choirs, teach classes, hold offices. They are affiliated with all the unfruitful works of darkness and never reprove them. If their hypocrisy is pointed out, they adopt the hush-hush policy by mis-using the admonition, "Judge not that ye be not judged," only another device of the devil to shut our mouths while the church moves into the Colosseum. We have long since ceased being disturbed by these sensitive souls who howl when the sword of the Spirit opens the pus-pockets of iniquity.

Living in Rome, we are tempted as never before to do as Rome does. When the church moves from perse-cution to popularity, from the arena into the grand-stand, the Gospel fire dies down until God starts an-other minority underground. He has followed this procedure through the centuries. Witness the Pilgrims, the Quakers, the Wesleyan movement. The church languishes when her members wear medals in the grandstand; she prospers when they wear scars in the arena. And be not deceived: what a lot of people think is the world becoming more Christian is the Christians becoming more worldly!

Furthermore, we have become enamored of the *showmanship* of the Colosseum. The time has come when sound doctrine cannot be endured, and, some-how, we have fallen for the notion that the church must compete with the world by entering the enter-tainment business. It is ridiculous to begin with, for we cannot begin to match the cleverness of this age by running third-rate amusements. It is an admission of failure and a sad commentary on present-day preach-ing when we must resort to numerous devices of music, movies, magic, and monkeyshines to fill the pews. It is contrary to the whole genius of the Christian message and ministry, for God ordained that men should be won by the foolishness of preaching, and when preaching fails there is no substitute. There are minor uses for lesser gifts, but the proclamation of the Gospel by Spirit-filled men is God's chosen means.

After all, "we are running a lifeboat and not a show-boat." But this is the age of the Colosseum, and not a few Christians think we must stage a glorified circus to keep step with these days of super-duper glamour.

It is the day of the spectator. Decadent Rome sat in the grandstand. America is a nation of onlookers to-day. Thousands upon thousands sit at football stadiums and baseball diamonds and horse races, watching man and beast strive for mastery. Then they go to the theater to be entertained again. Some of them go to church on Sunday and again they are spectators, not participants, and the preacher is expected to perform for their enjoyment. They go home with no more intention of practising the sermon than they take seriously what they saw in the theater. It is all unreal. Even Christians sit like the listeners of Ezekiel's day, hearing the Word but doing it not, and go out having deceived themselves. "Spectatoritis," whether in the amphitheater or at church, means a flabby generation of comfortable onlookers. For the church it spells decay. "I enjoyed the sermon" may be a sad index to the state of both pulpit and pew.

The church has moved from the catacombs to the Colosseum in its emphasis on *size*. We stage mammoth demonstrations and gigantic convocations. We put celebrities on the platform and borrow from Cæsar to enhance the banner of Christ. We have gone crazy over bigness. Just now church unification is the fashion. That is another admission of failure. Failing in the Spirit we are trying to impress men with size, as though strength lay in statistics. When the patient is very ill and the doctors hold a consultation, it does not mean only that the patient is up against it; it may mean that the doctors are up against it! We have gone on the defensive, forgetting that the best defensive is an offensive. If instead of all this banding together to make a show of strength, we secured a fresh filling of the Spirit and launched out with an aggressive evangelism we would win more souls in a week than we now win in a year. The fact is, the more we unify, the fewer souls are brought to Christ. The way out is by expansion, not by concentration. The saints of the catacombs did not sit in huddles and draw up resolutions deploring the *status quo*. They believed, lived, and preached the Gospel in the power of God, and empires gave way before them.

Actually, we need a thinning instead of a thickening. I learned long ago that growing corn and cotton must be thinned. We reduced the quantity to improve the quality. Gideon had to thin his troops, and a similar procedure might help God's army today. Jesus thinned His crowd, as recorded in the sixth chapter of John, and doubtless there was many another such occasion. Many believed on Him, we are told, but He did not believe in them. Today the persecuted minority has become the popular majority.

Real Christians, however, are still a minority in a pagan land right here in America. If instead of aping the world in *spirit, showmanship* and *size,* we returned to the offense of the cross and were willing to be the scum of the earth and a "theater to the world" in the New Testament sense instead of in the modern sense, we might once again shake the world. Men are not impressed from the Colosseum but from the catacombs. "Because the foolishness of God is wiser than men: and the weakness of God is stronger than men."

# 16

# The Victory of the Violent

*And from the days of John the Baptist until now the kingdom of heaven suffereth violence, and the violent take it by force.*

MATTHEW 11:12.

*The law and the prophets were until John: since that time the kingdom of God is preached, and every man presseth into it.*

LUKE 16:16.

THERE IS LITTLE AGREEMENT AMONG THE BIBLE SCHOLars on the meaning of this strange pronouncement of our Lord. Some think He meant that the kingdom of heaven as represented by the King and His disciples suffered violence at the hands of its enemies. Of course, that was true and is true to this day.

MacLaren thinks that Jesus referred to those who misunderstood the nature of the kingdom and were rudely rushing in with carnal enthusiasm as though it were an earthly realm, seeking to gain it by their own violence instead of by meekness, by arms and worldly force rather than by submission. Certainly we have always had these with us throughout the history of the church.

Is not this statement, however, really a picture, first of all, of the public reaction to the earthly ministry of our Lord? The multitudes were flocking to Jesus,

116

crowding like soldiers taking a fort. The rulers, the scribes, the Pharisees, the religionists, the Scripture scholars, stood aloof in their proud superiority, while the common people heard Him gladly and the rank and file thronged to hear His words. The very ones who should have been first to recognize Him never knew Him. Versed in prophecy, separated in conduct, punctilious in religious observance, more concerned over washing pots and pans than inward renewing, mistaking ritual for reality, they missed the kingdom, while publicans and harlots crowded in. Plain fishermen, beggars, tax-collectors, despised Samaritans, lepers, thieves, all these pressed in so desperately in earnest that they fairly stormed heaven. Bartimæus got his blessing. So did Zacchæus and the Syrophenician and the poor sick woman who elbowed through a crowd to touch Jesus. The centurion and the paralytic and the man born blind, what a motley mixture of unlikely prospects took the kingdom by force! And all the while the very teachers of the law who knew in advance when and how and where He was to come, His very own, knew Him not.

I say this text is a picture of our Lord's earthly ministry, and we do well to freshen our memory here. Do not think of Jesus standing in a pulpit droning platitudes to a few benchfuls of comfortable, sleepy saints. See Him outdoors, sunburned and plainly clad, teaching by the seaside or on the mountain top, while crowds of common folk hang on every word. See the scandalized scribes and Pharisees looking on, shaking their heads, critical of this new prophet, listening only to find something to grumble about. And while they size up the meeting from the sidelines, the blind see and the lame walk and the sick are healed and the lepers are cleansed and the dead are raised and the poor have the Gospel preached to them. What meetings they were! Of course, our Lord had preached in the synagogue, but it was not a very successful service. Out here, with the sky for a roof, everybody felt welcome, and they fairly stormed into the kingdom. The violent took it by force.

It began that way, and He who began to do and teach has been at it ever since, and the picture has been about the same down through the ages. Let us take a sample. Two hundred years ago Whitefield and Wesley stood outdoors in England and called the masses to repentance. And they came! They crowded into the kingdom, to the alarm of dignitaries and clergymen and the intelligentsia. Even good men misread the movement, like Rowland Hill, who said, "He [Wesley] and his lay lubbers go forth to poison the minds of men," and spoke of "Wesley's ragged legion of preaching tinkers, scavengers, draymen and chimney sweepers." The good brother had been horrified by the violent taking of the kingdom!

Of course, it had happened before, as in the days of Savonarola, and it was to happen again, as with Moody and nearer our own day under the rough tabernacles of Billy Sunday. The Welsh Revival saw grimy miners crowding with holy violence into the kingdom, while, for instance, G. Campbell Morgan sat enthralled to watch a revival without choir, songbooks, publicity, offerings, and sometimes without a preacher.

Verily, from the days of John the Baptist until this day every fresh Pentecostal outbreak has seen the kingdom of heaven suffer violence and the violent taking it by force. Around 1870 A. J. Gordon began his pastorate at Clarendon Street Baptist Church in Boston. It was an ivy-clad, sedate, closed corporation, so self-satisfied that an officer of the church was rebuked by a deacon for putting "Strangers Welcome" on some of the church circulars. A quartet choir in the gallery, which Gordon called the ice chest, furnished the music. Somebody called the church "The Saints' Everlasting Rest."

In the providence of God, D. L. Moody came to Boston in 1877 and pitched his tabernacle within three hundred feet of Gordon's church. Night after night for months he preached the plain Gospel to thousands of all ranks and conditions. Excursion trains brought in multitudes from all parts of New England. Seventy thousand homes in Boston were visited. Gordon's biographer writes:

At the center of these operations stood the Clarendon Street Church, like a cemetery temporarily occupied by troops in battle. What a shattering and overturning of weather-stained, moss-grown traditions followed! What experiences of grace, what widening vistas of God's power, what instruction in personal religion, resulted from these six months of revival! A new window was built into the religious life of the church, letting in floods of light. The true purpose of a church's existence began to be emphasized. Drunkards and outcasts were daily reclaimed, and brought into fellowship. . . . The entrance of reformed drunkards, and of all types of publicans and sinners, into membership opened the way for a progressive democratization culminating in the free-church system.

From "Adoniram Judson Gordon," by Ernest Gordon.

It was simply another repetition of our text: the kingdom of God was preached by Moody and the vio-

lent took it by force and every man pressed into it.
Clarendon Street Church was given a blood transfu-
sion of new life and a host of brand-new converts, the
best thing that can happen to any church. Out of it all
came a new church free of its fetters in the liberty
wherewith Christ makes us free.

Nothing better could take place in many a cold
church-sepulcher today than such an "outbreak of
violence," a mighty moving of God's Spirit sweeping
multitudes into the kingdom of God. Indeed, the recent outpourings of blessing in the Billy Graham meetings can be explained only in the light of our text. We
have witnessed the strange spectacle, which some said
would never be seen again, of throngs of publicans and
sinners crowding under vast tents and into stadiums,
and standing outdoors to hear the Gospel. We have
seen outcasts and movie actors and drunkards and
gamblers and racketeers taking the kingdom by force.
And such a sight has warmed the hearts of Christians,
until multitudes of all denominations who never
dreamed of worshiping together have sung and prayed
and wept and rejoiced under the power of God.

Make no mistake about it, when proud, cold, official,
organized Christianity quenches the free moving of
the Spirit, God will break out in a new place and use
converted rascals to preach the Gospel. And while
modern scribes and Pharisees, and sometimes Bible
scholars, sit aloof and look askance, the violent will
storm the kingdom and every man will press into it.
God does not blue-print His awakenings in our little
committee meetings. He may set aside our big projects
and programs and in His sovereign power raise up the
unlikeliest man and use the most unexpected means to

call to Himself one more crop of sinners before He rings the curtain down. God grant us one more "outbreak of violence" on the pattern of our text!

Years ago a convention met in Indianapolis to discuss "How to Reach the Masses." One day during that convention a young man stood on a box on a corner and began to preach. A crowd gathered, mostly workingmen going home to their suppers. They were electrified by the sermon. They forgot that they were tired. They forgot that they were hungry. The crowd became so dense that they had to move. The preacher announced that he would preach again at the Academy of Music. They followed him down the street and they filled the main floor of the building, sitting with their dinner buckets, while he preached again with such power that they were moved to tears. But he had only a few minutes to preach, because the convention on "How to Reach the Masses" was gathering in the same auditorium. While the convention was discussing how to reach the masses D. L. Moody was *doing* it! He was preaching the kingdom of God, and every man was pressing violently into it!

Such an "outbreak of violence" as our text sets forth is a godsend to any day and generation, for in the things of God *the victory goes to the violent.* I mean by that, the kingdom of heaven is possessed by those who are resolutely in earnest, who make it their chief concern. I am not preaching self-effort nor recognizing any merit in ourselves, for it is all the grace of God, but the Scriptures exhort us to strive to enter in at the strait gate, to labor to enter into God's rest, to give diligence to make our calling and election sure. God does business with those who mean business. There is a world of difference between leisurely walking down an aisle to join a church and desperately pressing through to Jesus. The preaching of this age has not disposed this generation to get very excited about going to heaven. Some Bible teaching has so minimized personal responsibility that any suggestion of effort on our part is frowned upon. To be sure, it is all of grace and the fight is a fight of faith, but it is still a fight and some saints could use a little sanctified violence to good profit. Why should we not be as desperately in earnest to possess our possessions in Christ as the world is to lay hold of all the devil has to offer? Joshua did not invade Canaan in a rocking chair and we do not take our Promised Land on a vacation jaunt. The saints of the ages have made the kingdom of God their absorbing passion, the main business of their lives. With them religion was not a side issue, a matter of an hour at church and a few dollars in a duplex envelope. Paul said, "To me to live is Christ," and to him Christ was just that, everything, life itself. This business of getting saved, living a Christian life and winning others, is a full-time occupation. We have to pray over it and weep over it and study over it and work over it, and if we possess it, it must possess us.

What we call revival is simply an outbreak of this sort of violence, when men and women desperately and resolutely press through to Jesus. The real enemies of revival are not the publicans and sinners. They were not the trouble-makers in Jesus' day. The real hindrance to revival is found in religious scribes who sit on the sidelines with their "i's" all dotted and their "t's" all crossed, who will have nothing to do with anything that does not speak their shibboleth. The real enemies of revival are those Pharisees who attend the meetings only to find fault, who are more concerned with form than force, more interested in ritual than in righteousness. The greatest foes of a real work of God are found among those prim, dainty, self-righteous folk who look on disdainfully, who are too refined and nice to touch a revival with a forty-foot pole, who say, "I am rich and increased with goods and have need of nothing," and who know not that they are wretched and miserable and poor and blind and naked. These poor souls are spectators, not participants, and they file the sermon away in convenient little mental cubbyholes, never dreaming that it was meant for them, seeing, as they do, everybody's sins but their own.

All these are successors to those onlookers of Jesus' day who stood by critically while the violent took the kingdom, and to all the spectators of the days of Wesley and Finney and Moody who smiled away the call of God or else stubbornly snubbed the Spirit. At any rate, whatever such may do today, I would ignore them just now to say to any sin-sick soul, "Come for yourself to the Saviour! Let no one keep you out of the kingdom. Make salvation your supreme interest and Christ your chief concern. Make it your one passion for the rest of your days to know Him and to make Him known. Join the ranks of the violent and take the kingdom by force. If it is worth anything it is worth everything. For Jesus paid it *all* and *all* to Him you owe.

> I am resolved to enter the kingdom,
> Leaving the paths of sin;
> Friends may oppose me, foes may beset me,
> Still will I enter in.

# 17

# *Strange Gods*

*We . . . preach unto you that ye should turn from these vanities unto the living God.*

ACTS 14:15.

*For they themselves shew of us what manner of entering in we had unto you, and how ye turned to God from idols to serve the living and true God.*

I THESSALONIANS 1:9.

IF A NATIVE CHRISTIAN SHOULD COME FROM HIS HEATHEN land to lecture to the saints in America he could easily make our faces red if he chose to speak on idols. He would find more strange gods here than he left behind him. We call our land Christian America and we thank God for all the advantages which we owe to Christianity, but, actually, true Christians in America are a minority group in a pagan land. There is no nation on earth where the first two of the Ten Commandments, to say nothing of the other eight, are broken daily by more people.

I heard a missionary say with telling effect that we have no right to give money and send missionaries to foreign lands to preach a Gospel which will cause commotion, divide homes, bring ostracism, suffering and even death, if we are not willing to pay a corresponding price over here. Over there it means giving up idols, and we have no right to hold on to ours.

God says, "Thou shalt have no other gods before me." An idol is someone or something we love more than we love God. America is a land of idolaters, not only outside the professing church, but inside it. We read of those who "feared the Lord, and served their own gods" (II Kings 17:33). Their number today is legion. Yet the Word of God tells us to "flee from idolatry" (I Cor. 10:14); asks, "What agreement hath the temple of God with idols?" (II Cor. 6:16), and commands, "Keep yourselves from idols" (I John 5:21). If we are to love God with all our heart, soul and mind, and if an idol is something we love more than we love God or something we love too much, then we must get rid of our idols if we are to love God as we ought.

When Jacob prepared to go back to Bethel, he said to his household and all that were with him, "Put away the strange gods that are among you" (Gen. 35:2). It is the first thing to do if we are going back to Bethel! When Gideon heard the call of God he threw down the altar of Baal. When Ephesus was awakened by Paul many brought their books of "curious arts" together and burned them in public. When men turn to God they turn from vanities and idols.

What are some of the strange gods today? We read of "the god of this world" (II Cor. 4:4), "the prince of this world" (John 12:31), "the prince of the power of the air, the spirit which now worketh in the children of disobedience" (Eph. 2:2). This present world system, politically, economically, socially, educationally, religiously, is under the devil and the whole world lies in the Wicked One. He is the god of most people, and plenty of church members pay him allegiance. Yet the Word of God tells us plainly not to love the world, or the things that are in the world, and that if we love the world, the love of the Father is not in us. This is not a Christian era, it is a pagan age and there are more heathen than ever. If Satan is the god of this age, then the love of this world system is idolatry.

Worldliness means far more than card playing, dancing, and theater going. It means being occupied with this world and its concerns to the exclusion or neglect of eternal issues. It means "eating and drinking, marrying and giving in marriage, buying and selling, planting and building," as in the days of Noah and Lot, until judgment overtakes us unprepared. "As it was in the days of Noah and Lot, so shall it be," said our Lord, and so it is now.

Just try being an out-and-out Christian in the present world of business, politics, society, economics, education, or even religion, and you will soon find out who runs it! Travel, as I have to do, in the midst of Sodom and Gomorrah, and you will find that this present set-up is not catering to Christians! I can remember a day, for instance, when smokers used to ask, "Does my smoking bother you?" Now, if it bothers, you can get off the train or out of the room! How often am I awakened on Pullmans in the middle of the night inhaling second-hand tobacco fumes from the pulmonary exhaust of some poor slave who, although the sign in the car expressly forbids it, must have his nicotine before morning! And since three out of four adults smoke, nobody pays much attention any more to the rights of the few who still do not use their noses for chimneys. Wade through the stench of beer and liquor and the blasphemy of both men and women in our public places, and you will soon realize that the millennium has not yet set in.

Try being a Christian in the world of education. No influence on earth has contributed more to the paganization of America than our Godless schools. There is still some Christian education to be had where Jesus Christ is still recognized on some college campuses, but the trend is away from God, not only in the secular schools but in many church schools founded to help perpetuate the Gospel but now become infidel factories and breeding grounds of atheism.

The god of this age and the ruler of this world set-up is Satan, and the lust of the flesh, the lust of the eyes, and the pride of life are still the supreme interests of men. We do not have a revival because our churches are filled with idolaters who cannot go up to Bethel, because they will not put away their strange gods. "Ye adulterers and adultresses, know ye not that the friendship of the world is enmity with God? Whosoever therefore will be a friend of the world is the enemy of God." When Christians love the world more than they love God, they are idolaters and adulterers, and we should be jealous for them with a godly jealousy, for they have been espoused to one husband and married to Christ.

Paul names another class of idolaters, numerous in these last days, "lovers of pleasures more than lovers of God" (II Tim. 3:4). Too many, even among our professing Christians, can play but cannot pray, know the names of the movie stars but cannot name the books of the Bible, can find Amos and Andy on the radio but would have trouble locating Amos and Andrew in the Bible. They know the baseball scores but not what the score is in God's Word. They yell like Comanche Indians at football games and sit like wooden Indians in church. They can weep over the glycerin tears of Hollywood divorcees and sit dry-eyed while missionaries plead for lost millions without God and without hope in this world.

The day is long gone when the movie was mere entertainment. Today it is a cult. The actors and actresses are actually called "idols," the theater is the church, the screen is the altar, the onlookers are the worshipers. It is idolatry in a vile and potent form.

We are told again that "the love of money is the root of all evil" (I Tim. 6:10). Add the rest of that verse and fill in the name of some Bible character who was ruined by money and see how it works out: "The love of money is the root of all evil: which while Achan, or Gehazi, or Balaam coveted after, he erred from the faith, and pierced himself through with many sorrows." How it fits! And how many it fits today! No wonder Paul says next, "But thou, O man of God, flee these things." The love of money gets into the pulpit, and while we would hardly expect a man to enter the ministry for money, he may worship Mammon before he gets out. The prophet sometimes turns racketeer and goes the way of Balaam. Others suppose that gain is godliness and make a lucrative business out of their Christian profession, advance their worldly interests by claiming to be Christians, and make piety a cloak for covetousness. "They imagine that religion is a paying concern" and that gain is godliness, which is contrary to what Paul teaches, that "godliness with con-

tentment is great gain. For we brought nothing into
this world, and it is certain we can carry nothing out."

The love of money gets into the church and we behold the modern counterpart of Abraham letting the
King of Sodom make him rich. It is a sad spectacle
when churches and denominations accept the gifts and
endowments of the world in spite of plain Scripture
that God's work must be supported by God's people
God's way. Ezra would not accept help from outsiders,
but the church has forgotten how to say "No" to the
subtle offers of the Adversary. The love of money is
idolatry, and the church of God, as well as the man of
God, will do well to "flee these things." The Word of
God teaches, not the denial of money on one hand or
its deification on the other, but its dedication, and if
there were fewer Christians worshiping the golden calf
there would be more rejoicing around the fatted calf
as prodigal sons come to God.

In Philippians Paul speaks of those whose god is
their physical appetites: "For many walk, of whom I
have told you often, and now tell you even weeping,
that they are the enemies of the cross of Christ: whose
end is destruction, whose god is their belly, and whose
glory is in their shame, who mind earthly things."
Now note the contrast: "For our conversation [citizen-
ship] is in heaven; from whence also we look for the
Saviour, the Lord Jesus Christ: who shall change our
vile body, that it may be fashioned like unto His glorious body, according to the working whereby he is able
even to subdue all things unto himself." In that day
the Greeks of the Epicurean philosophy enjoyed the
pleasures of the body and majored on it. Certainly,
the description fits the modern age with its glorifica-

tion of the physical, *"whose glory is in their shame."*
Over against that we are reminded that Christians are
a colony of heaven and that our conduct should befit
our citizenship.

We have let liberty run to license. Even stout fundamentalists who claim they want to hear God's Word
do not warm up to such passages that conflict with
their enjoyments. We are not legislating conduct, and
realize that what is considered good decorum in one
part of the country is frowned on in another. There is
a conscience on tobacco in one area, on movies in another, on mixed bathing in another. The tobacco user
resents bearing down on "filthiness" and too close an
application of verses about the body as the temple of
the Holy Spirit. Movie-goers would have you touch
lightly on "unfruitful works of darkness." And mixed
bathers who appear half clad pass quickly over that
verse about "modest apparel." Some of us still like to
see autumn come, when the saints are at least clothed
if not in their right minds!

Some appetites are natural and are to be governed
with temperance; others are acquired, and many of
them are to be denied with total abstinence. Any may
become gods and master us. The eater must put a knife
to his throat if given to appetite. Of course, from one
extreme in Philippians some run to the other in Colos-
sians. Faddists with a sprig of celery in one hand and a
leaf of lettuce in the other need to remember that
meats are to be received with thanksgiving, for every
creature of God is good and nothing to be refused if
it be received with thanksgiving, for it is sanctified by
the Word of God and prayer. Yet Christians do dig
their graves with their teeth, and McCheyne claimed

that the devil could defeat a preacher by making him a lover of good eating. Bunyan said the effect of many a sermon was ruined by a Sunday dinner. Were those old-timers too introspective and ascetic? Well, when a preacher really begins a closer walk with God, you will find him thumbing the pages of these old saints and not chumming with the happiness boys.

Certainly, the human body is the god of millions, and our hospitals, asylums and penitentiaries are filled with worshipers of the flesh. If you are a slave to any appetite you are an idolater. Put away your strange gods and go back to Bethel!

Our Lord said, "He that loveth father or mother, son or daughter, more than me is not worthy of me." Of course, most of us do not love our loved ones enough, but even at that, we may love them more than we love God. When Abraham offered Isaac, whatever else it proved, it showed that Isaac was not Abraham's god.

There is one other idol I would mention. Many a man who does not worship at any of the shrines I have mentioned goes into idolatry here. We are told that in the last days men will be "lovers of their own selves" (II Tim. 3:2). There is a sense in which we are to love ourselves, for we are to love our neighbors as ourselves, but many a man makes himself his god. A popular song used to run,

> I love me, I love me,
> I'm wild about myself.

Our Lord said that if we followed Him, we must deny *self*. The Macedonians first gave *themselves*. A man may renounce all other false deities and worship

at the shrine of self. It is the hardest idol to overthrow.
A lot of religious activity today is simply old Adam
operating under the auspices of the church. Ministerial
ambition, denominational pride, and the energy of
the flesh in general, try to do the work of the Spirit.
The egotist parades himself and calls it his testimony.
The gossip's tongue is as sharp as ever, only it is now
not criticism but "my honest opinion." Cover it up in
the language of the Gospel, perfume it with rhetoric,
throw in a few tears for effect, but when translated it
still reads,

> I love me, I love me,
> I'm wild about myself.

What is your idol? Put away the strange gods, turn
to God from idols. Turn from these vanities to serve
the living and true God.

> The dearest idol I have known,
> Whate'er that idol be,
> Help me to tear it from Thy throne
> And worship only Thee.

A missionary noticed in his congregation a native
clutching tightly in his hand an image of his idol. As
the speaker presented the Gospel, the hand gradually
relaxed, until with a soft thud the idol struck the floor.
Would that there might be a letting go of our idols in
the church these days!

> Lord Jesus, I long to be perfectly whole;
> I want Thee forever to live in my soul.
> *Break down every idol,* cast out every foe,
> Now wash me and I shall be whiter than snow.
>
> James Nicholson.

# 18

# Abounding Lawlessness and Abating Love

.

*And because iniquity shall abound, the love of many shall wax cold.*

MATTHEW 24:12.

THERE ARE THOSE WHO PREACH APLENTY FROM THE Sermon on the Mount—and well they may—but some of them grow strangely silent about the Olivet discourse. While we may differ as to some of the details, certainly a sermon that begins with the words, "Take heed that no man deceive you," was never meant to confuse but to clarify its subject.

Our Lord points out several things that "many" will be doing in the last days. Many shall be offended and shall betray and hate one another (v. 10). Many shall stumble, fall away, turn from Jesus, like Demas and Phygellus and Hermogenes long ago. Because persecution shall arise, many shall be offended. In another connection Jesus said, "Blessed is he whosoever shall not be offended in me." Our Lord is either a sanctuary or a stumbling stone and in the last days it will be easy to find in Him an occasion for stumbling.

False prophets shall arise and shall deceive many
(vs. 5, 11). Any religious ventriloquist with a dummy
can deceive a gullible generation that will not believe
the truth. Paul tells us that these deceivers will lead
captive silly women. Never have false teachers had such
a picnic leading astray the very people who boast of
their shrewdness.

But I am concerned just now with the third "many."
"And because iniquity shall abound, the love of many
shall wax cold." Here is a double-barreled description
of these times, and since "iniquity" means "lawlessness," what we have is Abounding Lawlessness and
Abating Love.

"Lawlessness shall abound." For further information, read any newspaper, listen to the radio, scan the
magazines, the best-sellers; just stand on any street corner and look and listen. Iniquity does not just exist; it
abounds. There is more of it than ever, it is more ex-
tensive and more excessive. Men love everything but
righteousness, and fear everything but God.

This lawlessness begins in the home, where "there
is a generation that curseth their father, and doth not
bless their mother" (Prov. 30:11). Paul tells us that
an outstanding mark of human depravity is disobedience to parents (Rom. 1:30), and it is also a mark of
the last days (II Tim. 3:2). Although at twelve years of
age our Lord could confound the wise men in the Temple, He returned to Nazareth, and "was subject" for
many years to Joseph and Mary. What a lesson for this
generation of young rebels thumbing their noses at
parental authority!

This lawlessness is fostered by modern pedagogy,
which frowns at discipline and would make obsolete

such words as "obedience" and "duty." Nothing must be allowed to thwart the personality development of the youngster, lest he be hampered, hindered, and inhibited. The dangers of repression are magnified, and self-expression is the big idea. These wiseacres forget that it is the steam repressed in the cylinders that drives the locomotive, not the steam expressed in the whistle.

So, what with no discipline at home or in school, we have a crop of juvenile delinquents and teen-age gangsters of the comic-book culture. The mystery of lawlessness that was already at work in Paul's day has honeycombed art and literature, business and society, religion and politics, and only the Restrainer, the Holy Spirit, keeps our world from being submerged in anarchy. When that restraint is removed, one might as well try to dam up Niagara Falls with toothpicks as to stem the tide of lawlessness now abounding.

Of course, it all springs from the corrupt human heart, deceitful and desperately wicked, and the carnal mind at enmity with God. Liberal theologians who laughed at sin a few years ago are now terrified by the wreck of this civilization, but still too proud to come clean and fully admit their heresy—even they must now acknowledge the truth of Romans 1 spread across every newspaper.

"Because iniquity shall abound, the love of many shall wax cold." With abounding lawlessness comes abating love. Observe that it is not zeal but love that waxes cold. Paul had zeal when he persecuted the church. One may give his goods to the poor and his body to be burned and have not love. Sardis had zeal, a name to be alive. Ephesus was aggressive and energetic, no doubt, but had left her first love.

Nor do we read that because lawlessness shall abound, the doctrine of many shall wax modernistic. It will, of course, but that is not what is in mind here. Some of the saints are as straight as a gun barrel doctrinally, and just as empty spiritually. Ephesus hated the deeds of the Nicolaitanes; her theology was sound. There are those who love to argue about the Abomination of Desolation and the Great Tribulation in this same chapter of our text but who seem to have overlooked this verse and are not grieved over their coldness of heart.

The sense of this verse is really that the love of most Christians will wax cold. Weymouth puts it: "Because of the spread of lawlessness the love of the great majority will grow cold." Moffatt has it, "And in most of you love will grow cold by the increase of iniquity." The new Revised Standard Version reads, "And because wickedness is multiplied, most men's love will grow cold." "When the Son of man cometh, shall He find faith on the earth?" Certainly He will not find much love.

We are living in a strange and weird hour. A sinister and satanic atmosphere pervades the world. The god of this age knows that his time is short and that the powers of darkness are working overtime. The lines are drawn, the issue is Christ or Antichrist, and we have on one hand a demonstration of the Spirit and on the other a "*demon*-stration" of the devil.

It is a tired and weary world. The journey is too great for us all. Men's hearts fail them for fear. On top of the physical and mental languor there is poured out a spirit of deep sleep. Satan is out to disable the body, deceive the mind, and discourage the spirit. He tells sinners they are safe and he tells saints they are lost.

In such an hour it is not easy to keep the heart-fires burning. I have discovered Christians whom I have known for years gradually cooling off in their love toward God. Often in Christian homes it is difficult to talk on spiritual things. Talk anything else, and it would take several shorthand experts to keep up with the conversation; talk of Christ and one would think he was sitting up with a corpse.

When love toward Christ abates, love of the brethren dies. This badge by which we know that we have passed from death to life and by which all men know that we are His disciples is conspicuous for its absence. Another Tertullian could never write that it is said of us, "How those Christians love each other!" If the man who says he loves God and hates his brother is a liar we have a bumper crop.

When love toward God abates, we begin to love what we ought to hate. Prayer-meetings become a drudgery and the movies a delight. We say of the house of God, as did the people of Malachi's day, "Behold, what a weariness is it!" When we love God we hate sin, we abhor that which is evil, we abstain from the very appearance of evil. "The fear of the Lord is to hate evil." "If any man love the world, the love of the Father is not in him." We have lost our sensitiveness to sin. We have become tolerant of evil. We say, "Oh, well, things are not so bad; they could be worse." We think it a mark of broadmindedness to grow lenient toward sin, when actually it means that our love has grown cold.

Here is a test of our spiritual state: Do I now allow

what once I abhorred? When the love of God abates, love of evil abounds. The man who tolerates sin will soon endorse and practise sin.

Has your love died down? Then stir up the gift of God that is within you. Repent and pray that the love of God may be shed afresh in your heart by the Holy Spirit. Jesus asked Peter, "Lovest thou me?" Everything else stems from that. When we love Him we will love the sheep and we will feed the sheep and we will go after lost sheep.

In Scotland years ago, before matches were invented, the fires went out in a certain community. The neighbors began to search for a house where smoke still curled from a chimney. Finally, on a hillside they found one little cottage where the fire still burned. Presently they came from all around to get a shovelful of coals to carry back to their own blackened hearths, and after a while the cheerful flames burned all over the neighborhood.

The fires are going out all over the world today. Keep your heart-fires burning, and others will be drawn by your warmth to seek coals for their own heart-fires. If the ashes have accumulated, get rid of them and stir up God's gift within you. Beware of abounding lawlessness and abating love!

# 19

# Gamaliel, the Appeaser

NOBODY EVER CALLED THE ACTS OF THE APOSTLES A DULL
book. Something is happening in it every minute.
These early Christians, on fire for God, tackled the
world, the flesh and the devil in a head-on collision
and soon got into plenty of trouble.

By the time we reach the fifth chapter this trouble
has assumed several forms. The chapter begins with
trouble inside the church: "But a certain man named
Ananias, with Sapphira his wife . . ." The church has
always been harmed most by trouble within, but at this
time it was not so anemic as now and the poison was
soon cleared.

Then trouble looms again on the outside. Peter and
the apostles are again brought before the council, the
religious authorities. True Christianity through the
ages has always clashed with organized religion. Peter
and the apostles minced no words. Their speech is a
classic: "We ought to obey God rather than men. The
God of our fathers raised up Jesus, whom ye slew and
hanged on a tree. Him hath God exalted with his right
hand to be a Prince and a Saviour, for to give repentance to Israel, and forgiveness of sins. And we are his

witnesses of these things; and so is also the Holy Ghost, whom God hath given to them that obey him."

No wonder the council was "cut to the heart"! A sermon like that, with the Trinity in it, Calvary in it, the resurrection in it, repentance in it, forgiveness in it, the gift of the Spirit in it, plainly charging the rulers with murder and boldly claiming to be Christ's witnesses—and all in four verses!—a sermon like that was bound to cut to the heart even a religious council, often the hardest crowd on earth to move.

Trouble within, trouble without. And now comes another kind of trouble in disguise, trouble on the fence. Dr. Gamaliel, learned and famous teacher of the law, stands up. He cautions them to be careful what they do with these men. He cites two cases on record, two men, Theudas and Judas, who had led popular movements that came to nought. He advised suspended judgment. "If this counsel or this work be of men it will come to nought: but if it be of God, ye cannot overthrow it; lest haply ye be found even to fight against God."

There was a time when I was much impressed with Gamaliel. I thought he made a great speech. It sounded sober, sane and sound, level-headed, reasonable. But the years have changed my convictions about many men, and I have had a radical change of mind about Gamaliel.

The fact is, Gamaliel was an appeaser and he compromised this meeting into a Munich. If Peter was an apostle of Christ, Gamaliel was an apostle of compromise. He was one of the first protagonists of that tolerance which has disgraced the pages of history through the centuries.

There is no excuse for Gamaliel. He was a teacher in Israel and knew these things. He knew the Scriptures about Jesus Christ. And Jesus Christ had come and fulfilled these Scriptures right in Gamaliel's vicinity and in his time, for this thing was not done in a corner. It was no time for suspended judgment. There was nothing to suspend judgment about. Gamaliel should have taken his stand with these apostles. There is a tradition that he became a Christian, but it is more likely that he lived and died a Pharisee. It is to his eternal disgrace that, like Meroz, he came not to the help of the Lord against the mighty. Of course, there would have been a price to pay if he, a teacher in reputation, had taken his stand with these despised Galileans. Gamaliel decided to be neither for nor against. He took to the fence, and there he sits as the first of a line of straddlers who have perhaps caused the church more trouble than trouble within or trouble without. God would rather have a man on the wrong side of the fence than *on* the fence. The worst enemies of apostles are not the opposers but the appeasers.

Gamaliel made three mistakes. First, he *made a false comparison*. Although the apostles were immediately in mind, he was really comparing Jesus Christ with Theudas and Judas, for it was Jesus who had started this movement. But you cannot compare Jesus with Theudas or Judas or anybody else. Jesus Christ is Jesus Christ. He admits of no comparison. There is a popular tendency today to airily measure Jesus in the same mold one uses for ordinary men and to compare the Christian movement with man-made religions and enterprises. Some of it has a very scholarly smell and sounds as though it were honest, but it is utterly beside the point. Paul wasted no time comparing the Gospel with current religions and trying to convince his hearers that the Gospel was the best answer to the world's ills that had as yet come along. He declared it to be the only answer that ever had come along or ever would come along, all in a class to itself, with all comparisons out of order. Jesus Christ is Jesus Christ, the first and last. Without Him nothing can be done about salvation. With Him nothing more need be done. Theudas and Judas and all men and movements may be compared with each other but never with Him. God has spoken, God has come, God lived and died and rose again in His Son. That is finality, and all Gamaliels who try to liken something else or someone else to Jesus Christ are trying to compare the incomparable.

Furthermore, Gamaliel *suggested a false criterion.* "We will measure this movement by the success of it. Time will tell." Now, success may be the standard gauge of this world, and "nothing succeeds like success," but earth's yardstick does not apply to Jesus Christ. According to the viewpoint of His time Jesus was a failure. He died in disgrace, the death of a criminal, and His followers were scattered. Nineteen centuries have gone, and today it still looks as though Cæsar, not Christ, were on the throne and that the world, the flesh and the devil had things pretty much their way. And, instead of the world being converted, we know that the Lord Himself said, "When the Son of man cometh, shall he find faith on the earth?" That certainly is not success as this world measures it. Nor is it true in the things of Christ that "time will tell." But eternity will tell and we await the verdict of eternity.

The man who postpones taking his stand for Jesus Christ until he sees how the Gospel movement succeeds will live and die with Gamaliel. Visible success has never been the proof of Jesus or His followers. They have been the scum and offscouring of the earth, and although God often blesses true Christians with wealth and advancement in things material, all that is purely incidental. He who tries to use this world's textbooks on success in the things of the Spirit will end up like the man who offered to sell a set of books on "How to Succeed" for a month's room and board! It just doesn't work.

Finally, Gamaliel *arrived at a false conclusion.* "Refrain from these men, and let them alone." But you can't let them alone! You cannot play hands off with the cause of Jesus Christ. "He that is not with me is against me; and he that gathereth not with me scattereth abroad." You cannot suspend judgment and do nothing. You are either dead or alive, and you are either a Christian or you are not. This polite business of waiting to see how it all turns out, adding up all the evidence and making up our minds later when we think all the facts are in, puts man on the pedestal and Jesus before him on trial in the hope of meriting His approval. The fact is, we are guilty and condemned sinners, with the wrath of God abiding on us but with mercy offered, and until we definitely trust Christ we have definitely rejected Him. "He that believeth on him is not condemned: but he that believeth not is condemned already, because he hath not believed in the name of the only begotten Son of God." That admits of no fence-sitters, although many would assume such a position. You cannot leave Jesus Christ or His cause alone. You are with Him or against Him, gathering or scattering, condemned or not condemned.

So Gamaliel was utterly mistaken in what seems at first thought a sound and sane position. He was right when he said that if the Gospel movement were of men it would come to nought but if it were of God it could not be overthrown. But if we get no further than all those "ifs" we shall die in our sins. Until we decide that it is of God and join it, we oppose it. It is we who are on trial. There was a man in a European art gallery who criticized the pictures severely as he walked out the door. The old doorkeeper replied, "If you please, sir, the pictures are no longer on trial but the spectators are!" Christ and the Gospel have proven themselves, and who are we to take the judges' seat and pass on them? God offers salvation as a free gift: take it and you are saved; leave it and you are lost. And until you take it, you leave it.

But Gamaliel's stand reaches out into many applications. As we said at the outset, he was an appeaser, an opportunist, who would not commit himself. We are reminded of the crowd on Carmel when Elijah called down fire from heaven. There were seven thousand in Israel who had not bowed to Baal. There were four hundred and fifty priests of Baal. Both of these groups had at least taken a stand and could be numbered. But when Elijah challenged his congregation, "How long halt ye between two opinions? If the Lord be God, follow him: but if Baal, then follow him," we read that "the people answered him not a word." They would not commit themselves. They would not take a stand. They would wait and see how things turned out.

This is an age of appeasement. It begins in the home,

where the rod is spared and the child spoiled. It continues in school, where right and wrong have become relative instead of absolute. It shows up in nations as it did at Munich. And it has infected the professing church. It does not take a clear stand with Peter and in no uncertain words cut the opposition to the heart. It straddles the fence with Gamaliel and dismisses the assembly.

Erasmus was a typical appeaser, in true succession to Gamaliel. It has been written:

> He [Luther] dwells on the ingenious carefulness of Erasmus to avoid decisive utterance, attempting always to shade down his Yes till it is almost a No, and to burnish up his No until it might almost pass for a Yes. Erasmus is a Proteus! He is an eel. . . . In the debate . . . people of academic culture, of speculative disengagement and serene intellectual indifference, sided with Erasmus. The Moderates throughout Europe, the gentlemen of courts, the semi-skeptical intelligences of the universities, told the golden-mouthed apostle of compromise that he was in the right. . . . The heart of Christianity beat with Luther instead.

This is the age of Gamaliel and Erasmus, when, in the name of tolerance, men halt between two opinions and answer not a word. In the church it shows up in Laodicean lukewarmness, a little too hot to be cold and a little too cold to be hot, a state that nauseates the Lord Himself. The Gospel usually makes men mad, sad or glad, but today we walk out of our churches neither sad, mad nor glad—we just walk out. It were better that we went out mad! Gamaliel was neither. Peter was glad in the Lord, and his audience was mad, but Gamaliel was Gamaliel, just tolerant and nothing more.

Such a spirit shows up in our pulpits, where Gamaliels flourish and apostles are few. Joseph Parker, writing about Nathan the prophet, who told King David, "Thou art the man," says:

Definite statements are manageable but vague charges are never to be entertained. He is always a false accuser who makes a general charge; he is a learned false witness skilled and cunning who says he will not go into the case; he will say nothing about it; he thinks it better to hold his tongue. Would God his tongue had been cut when he said that! He has said more by not saying than he could have if he had told the truth. . . . No man makes progress who deals in generalities.

But Nathan belongs to the category of Peter and John and John the Baptist and Paul and Luther—and the Lord of them all. The issue is too clear-cut for middle-of-the-roaders, fundamental modernists and modernistic fundamentalists, neither fish nor fowl. The issues are life and death, heaven and hell, and the case does not call for suspended judgment.

The devil never had a greater ally than this modern atmosphere of genial, amiable, pleasant tolerance, in which nothing is bad, everything is good, and black and white are smeared into an indefinite gray. Nothing matters if everybody is in good humor. Let us not get excited over Peter and John and their Jesus. We will not stoop to take sides. We will see how it works out. Well, the church is still marching on, but nobody ever got anywhere with Gamaliel. Getting mixed up with an unpopular movement is not the worst thing one can do. I would rather have lost my head with James than have kept it with Gamaliel. This modern brand of tolerance has put our age into a stupor. Nothing is important enough to contend for. The devil does great business when the moral sensibilities of men have thus been doped. Even beer ads make much of this "America of kindliness, of friendship, of good-humored tolerance." Well did Gresham Machen say that "the most important things are not those about which men are agreed but those for which men will fight." But the fatigue and languor of this age have got us. Everybody is too dead tired to line up with Peter and the Gospel. It is much more comfortable to suspend judgment and go home to bed.

To be sure, some men have made mistakes on the side of Peter and the Gospel. Peter made some himself. But he never made the supreme mistake of waiting to follow Jesus until he saw how it all turned out. He threw his blundering impetuous self into the Saviour's cause from the very beginning, and although for a while almost everything he said and did was a mistake, his heart was not on the fence. He even denied his Lord, but he came back. The other disciples, too, forsook their Lord and fled. But they ended up, all but Judas, faithful through prison and scourging and martyrdom or lonely exile. They paid the price. Down through the centuries a worthy succession has followed in their train. And along the road they have evermore met their opposers within and without. But the church has never suffered from antagonism half as much as from appeasement. The apostles have had their opposers, but a thousand times more dangerous have been the appeasers.

We can thank God that Gamaliel had one pupil who did not follow in his steps. Paul started out an opposer and ended an apostle, but he never disgraced his name

as an appeaser. You could always tell which side of the
fence was Paul's. He was on either side with a vengeance. When he was against Christ, he was against Him.
When he was for Him, he was for Him. He never sat
on the fence with his famous teacher. Paul never could
forget that he had opposed the church, but he never
had to confess that he appeased the opposition. The
opposition slew him, but he outlived it just the same.
God help us to follow him as he followed Christ!

# 20

# *"Unless the Spirit"*

*Not by might, nor by power, but by my spirit, saith the Lord of hosts.*

ZECHARIAH 4:6.

BACK IN THE RUSTIC RURAL COMMUNITY OF MY BOYHOOD days we used to sing an old-fashioned song character-istic of the period before the Age of Amen gave way to the Era of So What? It ran like this:

> Brethren, we have met to worship
> And adore the Lord our God;
> Won't you pray with all your power
> While we try to preach the Word?
> All is vain unless the Spirit
> Of the Holy One come down;
> Brethren, pray and holy manna
> Will be showered all around.

> From "Brethren, We Have Met
> To Worship," by Geo. Atkins.

I like especially that line, "All is vain *unless the Spirit . . .*"

The plight of many churches is summed up in the words spoken to Jesus by the father who brought his demonized boy to the disciples at the foot of the Mount of Transfiguration: "I besought thy disciples to cast him out; *and they could not.*" We are powerless before a demonized world. And it is not because we do not have knowledge, equipment, programs, activity, money. Never has the church had more—and less!

Missionaries tell us that sometimes chimpanzees imitate them by gathering wood and arranging it for a fire—but they do not know how to produce the fire. The church has her wood in excellent order today. The system is perfect, but—we have no fire.

The Old Testament tells us how Elisha sent Gehazi, his servant, to raise the Shunammite's son. He carried the prophet's staff and observed the prophet's orders, "but there was neither voice nor hearing." Today Gehazi goes about at Elisha's orders, carrying Elisha's staff, but although he goes through the prescribed motions the dead do not come to life. Although we say all the words the demons do not depart.

Never has the church had more wire stretched with less power in it. "All is vain *unless the Spirit* of the Holy One come down." Sad to say, we seem not even to know that we have not the Spirit in power. If He ceased His work many church members would never know the difference. Like Samson, we wist not that He has departed, but we keep "shaking ourselves" in the prescribed calisthenics.

Such was the sad plight of the churches in Asia to which our Lord spoke in Revelation. Ephesus was loveless and didn't know it. Sardis was lifeless and didn't know it. Laodicea was lukewarm and didn't know it. "Thou sayest . . . and knowest not" is descriptive of altogether too many churches today. In any case "all is vain *unless the Spirit* . . ."

We go to extremes, we either freeze or fry. Some services are too formal and we come out like ramrods, having mistaken spiritual *rigor mortis* for dignity. We ought to be dogmatic plus but sometimes we are dogmatic—period. So are there other fellowships coldly orthodox, having the facts but no fire. Again, we sometimes go to the other extreme, where we sit through a frenzy of evangelistic epilepsy and come out nervous, feeling more as if we had been to a circus than to a church. In either case, "all is vain *unless the Spirit . . .*"

We do not have to choose between freezing or frying. Certainly, most of the saints do need defrosting. One thing can stop Niagara—it can freeze! The same trouble stops many a church. Deep-freeze lockers are nothing new: we have had them on street corners with steeples on top for years.

We could stand a little emotion nowadays. The World Series baseball games almost stop business in many a section of our land, so intense is the interest. If a revival so interfered with our normal processes you would hear the complaint that we were going crazy. Indeed, that was a complaint made during the Welsh Revival. A spell of that kind of insanity would be welcome, "think" some of us who have grown weary of the present insanity misnamed progress.

We have already referred to Samson, who wist not when the Spirit of the Lord departed from him. There was a time when the Spirit was with him. It is stated in a most interesting fashion: "And the Spirit of the Lord came mightily upon him . . . and he had nothing in his hand" (Judges 14:5, 6). Nothing in his hand! We have too many things in our hands today, carnal weapons of our own choosing, and even God cannot fill what is already full. It was the invisible weapon that prevailed in Samson's case, as with Gideon and his "sword of the

Lord." God wants us empty-handed when we go out, that we may be full-handed when we come in. Samson's hands were filled with honey for himself and others. When life is done, we want to go home full-handed: "Shall I go and empty-handed?" we sing, and the answer is "No." But the Spirit of God comes mightily on those who have nothing in their own hands, that He may fill their hands forevermore.

We are in serious danger of forgetting that it is not by might or by power but by the Spirit of the Lord of hosts. We cannot meet the Goliath of this age in Saul's armor. When we try to grapple with the adversary in unsanctified strength we throw away our only chance of success. The Bible is one long record of men and women who dared to be utterly ridiculous in order to prove God. Abraham, the priests at Jericho, Gideon, David facing Goliath, these and many more dared to make the glorious venture where "all is vain unless the Spirit" comes to one's aid. If it hadn't worked they would have been laughing-stocks to all subsequent generations. But it worked!

Today we are afraid to prove God. We borrow the world's program and pep and propaganda and paraphernalia and personnel. But from the world we cannot borrow power, the power that works the works of God. Our efficiency turns out to be deficiency unless we have His sufficiency. We have a name to be alive as had Sardis, but we merely double our activities to hide our weakness. "It is not conquering energy conscious of its power but feverish energy conscious of its powerlessness." We have developed in Christian work the go-getter salesman type who "goes" more than he "gets," hunches over tables in cafeterias "making contacts" instead of getting on his knees talking to God. And all our modern St. Vitus's dance merely reveals the fact that we have not the Spirit.

There are others who sense their lack of power and set about in diverse ways to improve matters. They introduce this innovation, dispense with that, a mere reshuffling of arrangements; but the church is as powerless before the demons as ever. Rules upon rules are invented, but the sorriest hotel usually posts the most regulations, and the same holds for churches.

What to do? I suggest no "steps." There are books of them already in circulation. Until we are really convicted of our need, humble enough to acknowledge it and desperate enough to lay hold upon God, we shall continue like Gehazi to go through all the motions in vain. And when we are so convicted and humble and desperate we will get through to God. The best way to learn how to pray is to pray, and the man who really hungers and thirsts for God will need no "steps" to satisfy his soul.

"All is vain unless the Spirit . . ." Let us pray as we ought, and "holy manna will be showered all around."

# 21

# *Pattern for Perilous Times*

PAUL, THE VETERAN APOSTLE, IS NEARING THE END OF his race. He has run it with patience, and now he is about to pass the torch to his son in the Gospel, Timothy. It is a fine thing when a minister has a son of his own who is also a son in the Gospel, but if he has no son in the flesh he may have one in the faith.

Paul is helping Timothy to get his bearings. He tells Timothy that the time will come when men will not endure sound doctrine. He was under no illusions about the future. He had told the elders of Ephesus that after his departing, grievous wolves would enter in, not sparing the flock, and that within the church false leaders would arise (Acts 20:29–30). Some preachers today would never think of warning against false doctrine. They say it is the wrong approach, is not psychologically correct, that we should be optimistic about the future. If such procedure is wrong, then the New Testament is wrong in a lot of places.

Paul said the time would come "when they can't take it," and that time has arrived. The Gospel message is foolishness to this world, of course, and, incidentally, if the message be foolishness what can the messengers expect but to be called fools? But the time has come when the church cannot endure sound doctrine, not

154

the liberals alone, but plenty of fundamentalists. Alexander Whyte spoke of those who "will be thankful to you for telling them the particular times when the Gospels were writ or for explaining the meaning of Euroclydon or anathema maranatha. They will be glad," said he, "for such useless instruction. But if you touch upon such subjects as try the state and way of their lives, these religious people cannot bear to be thus instructed."

In such a time what is the preacher to do? "But watch thou in all things, endure afflictions, do the work of an evangelist, make full proof of thy ministry." He is to be a "gospelizer" and if the people won't endure it, preach it anyway! Such was the charge given to Isaiah and Jeremiah. Read the second chapter of Ezekiel. The prophet was to face an impudent, stiff-hearted and rebellious people and not be afraid of them, but "whether they will hear, or whether they will forbear," he was to speak God's words until they should know that a prophet had been among them.

I have already mentioned Alexander Whyte. One would think that after eighty a minister would face no more crises in his ministry. But in his old age Dr. Whyte wrestled with the question whether he should for the remainder of his ministry preach more on the gentler and more hopeful aspects of Christian truth and less on sin and its fruits. He says:

What seemed to me to be a Divine Voice spoke with all-commanding power in my conscience, and said to me as clear as clear could be: "No! Go on, and flinch not! Go back and boldly finish the work that has been given you to do. Speak out and fear not. Make them at any cost to see themselves in God's holy Law as in a glass. Do you that, for no one else will do it. No one else will so risk his life and his reputation as to do it. And you have not much of either left to risk. Go home and spend what is left of your life in your appointed task of showing my people their sin and their need of my salvation."

It is not easy to keep a charge like that in a day like this. We have heard of an army officer in the thick of a battle who called to his superior and said, "The flag has been carried 'way ahead of the regiment. Shall we bring it back?" His superior thundered back, "No! Make the regiment catch up with the flag!" The tendency today is to bring our flag back to our faltering battle lines. We need to bring the regiment up with the flag.

If we are to be faithful in such a time let us remember that there is *a price to pay*. "Endure afflictions," is Paul's word to Timothy. He was to endure hardness as a good soldier of Jesus Christ. Paul knew from experience. He had suffered the loss of all things, had endured hardship and suffering.

It costs us nothing to be saved. Eternal life is the gift of God. It cost God aplenty. It cost our Saviour His life, but it is free to us. But if we are to be soldiers of the cross and followers of the Lamb, it will cost us everything we have and we shall be in for plenty of trouble.

The preacher who stands for God and righteousness and exposes sin thereby "sticks his neck out," and becomes the target of all the subtle and sinister attacks of the Adversary. Sometimes we dodge the issue by deciding to specialize in a ministry of comfort. Dr. John Watson felt in his late years that if he had his life to live over, he would give himself more to such a ministry. But John Henry Newman said, "Those who make comfort the great subject of their preaching seem to mistake the end of their ministry. *Holiness is the great end,* comfort is a cordial, but no one drinks cordials from morning to night." It is easier to comfort the afflicted than to afflict the comfortable, but there is need for both.

Noah had no converts and perhaps it was because he was "a preacher of righteousness." People do not like to be called to holiness and righteousness and will not flock to the prophet who calls to a straight and narrow way. It costs to do that kind of preaching. It costs in popularity. There is a mistaken notion that the world will honor the man who stands for God. It will break his neck if it can. Jesus said they hated Him and would hate us. Our Lord had a crowd at the beginning of His ministry. They came to Him from every quarter, and His disciples said, "All men seek for thee." But there came a day when even His disciples forsook Him and fled.

Sometimes it costs at home. A man's foes may be those of his own household. When Sam Jones entered the ministry his wife told him she had married a lawyer, not a preacher, and would never be a Methodist minister's wife. Sam told her he would preach the Gospel if he had to travel as a grass widower. The night before he left for Conference she was taken violently ill. She had said that if Sam became a preacher she would have to be removed first. It looked as if she were going to be removed. She promised God then and there that if He would save her life she would be the best preacher's wife she knew how to be. She recovered and kept her promise. God mightily used Sam

Jones all over America because he was ready to pay the price.

There is a price to pay in loneliness. Look at Paul in the fourth chapter of Second Timothy. He calls the roll of his friends, and most of them are conspicuous for their absence. Demas had forsaken him, having loved this present world. Crescens had gone to Galatia, Titus to Dalmatia. Tychicus had been sent to Ephesus. Paul needs his cloak and parchments. Alexander the coppersmith has done him much evil. "At my first answer no man stood with me," he says. Does not that remind you of Another of whom we read "And all his disciples forsook him and fled"? But Paul does not end here: "Notwithstanding the Lord stood with me and strengthened me." There is not only *a price to pay*, there is *a promise to plead*.

God has said, "I will never leave thee nor forsake thee," and so precious is that word that it shows up in Genesis and Deuteronomy and Joshua and the Psalms and Isaiah and Hebrews. Our Lord has said, "Lo, I am with you always, even unto the end of the age." If we pay the price, we can plead the promise.

I started out ten years ago to travel over this land in an itinerant ministry under no particular auspices or sponsorship. The devil said, "You mean well, but the religious world is so organized today that you will have to pull a few wires and get under somebody's wing in order to keep going. If you preach plainly they won't receive it and you'll starve." Well, I may look as if I am starving but I am not. I have had three meals every day, and God has gone before and opened doors I couldn't have entered with a crowbar. I turned my reputation, my calls, my future over to the Lord, and He has never left me nor forsaken me.

> Got any rivers you think are uncrossable?
> Got any mountains you cannot tunnel through?
> God specializes in things thought impossible;
> And He will do what no man can ever do.

"I will never leave thee nor forsake thee." One thinks of the old lady whose pastor tried to explain that the verse could really mean, "I'll never, never, never forsake thee." She replied, "The Lord may have to say it three times to get you Greek scholars to believe it, but once is enough for me."

Not only is there *a price to pay* and *a promise to plead,* there is *a prize to possess.* "Henceforth there is laid up for me a crown of righteousness, which the Lord, the righteous judge shall give me at that day: *and not to me only,* but unto *all them also that love his appearing.*" We are to so run *that we may obtain.* I don't want the booby prize when I get to heaven. There is for us the prize of the high calling of God in Christ Jesus, and we are to let nothing take our crown. Discouragement can do it: Elijah almost lost his under a juniper. Success can do it: David almost lost his in a king's palace. The wrong kind of books can do it. Eating and drinking can do it. We can be so busy even with the good that we miss the best in a round of glorified piddling. The fear of man can do it. Ecclesiastical pressure can do it. The wrong school can do it. "Look to yourself, that we lose not those things which we have wrought, but that we receive a full reward."

Some of the saints seem so smug in positional truth

that it doesn't matter to them whether they receive a reward or not. Indeed, we do not work to get to heaven, but rewards will be handed out at the judgment seat of Christ, and I don't want to miss anything God has for me, nor do I want to let the devil cheat me out of my crown.

Paul wanted to finish his course with joy (Acts 20: 24). We are never safe in that respect until the last step. Some who started gloriously ran well until within sight of the goal, only to finish miserably. It may have been money or morals or modernism. What fools we can be on the home stretch! No wonder a dear old saint prayed, "Lord, keep me from being a wicked old man!"

Paul ran well, but he kept his body under subjection, lest, having preached to others, he himself should be a castaway. He ran with patience, looking unto Jesus, who for the joy that was set before Him endured the cross, despising the shame, and is set down at the right hand of the throne of God. He won His prize! Let us consider Him, lest we be weary and faint in our minds. And considering Him, let us pay the price and plead the promise and possess the prize.